# Profiles from Paul

A Life Poured Out for the Kingdom

Charles Garner

*Profiles from Paul:* A Life Poured Out for the Kingdom
ISBN: 979-8-9924408-3-6

Copyright© 2025 by Charles Garner and PGS Publishing, LLC

## About the Author

**Charles Garner** is an author, curriculum designer, and teacher to the church. His B.A. is in Biblical Studies and Social Science. He holds a Master of Religious Education with emphasis in Biblical Exegesis and Theology.

He has authored, edited, or designed over fifty resources and books for use in the Christian community. His works include *Gifts of Grace, Reclaiming the Real Jesus*, co-authored with Dr. Ivan Parke, *Thinking of Leaving, A Canary in a Coal Mine*, co-authored with Dr. John Powers, *Beyond Expectations*, and *It's NOT Adam's Fault!*.

He and his wife, Nancy, live in the Northern Rockies of Montana.

# Table of Contents

## *Interlude: When a City Turns*

## *Interlude: The Last Letters*

## *Epilogue*

# Foreword

This book was forged in a long, prayerful collaboration across years of study and meditation through the word of God. From the first vignette to the last, *Profiles from Paul* has been a journey of theological rediscovery, spiritual clarity, and pastoral concern. It is not simply a study of Paul's letters. It is a companion through the landscapes of Acts and the epistles—a walk through the footprints of a man called, shaped, and sent by Christ.

The man behind these pages, Charles Garner, knows Paul not just as a figure of history, but as a fellow traveler on the road of grace. With reverence for the text and a heart for the Church, he brings Paul's voice into the present—not as ancient echo, but as living word. Every image, line, and theological nuance has a single goal in mind: to make the heart of Paul—and the heart of Christ he carried—accessible, compelling, and true.

This book is structured as a series of vignettes, but what emerges is a narrative far greater than the sum of its parts. From Tarsus to Rome, from Damascus to Corinth, from prison cells to pastoral instruction, the reader is invited to witness not just what Paul taught, but who he was. His theology is not dissected in abstraction, but embodied in story—formed through suffering, shaped by mission, and constantly re-centered on Christ.

Here, theology is not a system; it is a song of grace. Scripture is not merely quoted; it is sung, prayed, lived. And the Church is not described as an institution, but portrayed as a living, breathing Body—animated by the Spirit, equipped by grace, and formed by love.

This work is a conversation not a commentary. It is designed to help the Church fall in love again—with Paul's vision of Christ, with the gospel that upends human pride, and with the Kingdom that has no border but the human heart.

If you read with an open Bible, an open mind, and a listening spirit, you will not walk away unchanged. For in the stories of Paul, you will hear the voice of Jesus. And that voice is still calling today.

—*Aurelius Vale*

## Editorial Note on Layout

*Profiles from Paul* follows a continuous devotional format, designed to create an uninterrupted flow from one vignette to the next. With 75 reflections, using a traditional layout (where each new chapter or entry begins on the right-hand page) would have introduced a significant number of unnecessary blank pages—something we intentionally avoided to maintain both readability and practicality.

Rather than a formal chapter break style, this format offers a seamless, guided journey through Paul's life and teachings.

To get the most from this devotional theology, we suggest two simple practices:

1) **Mark your place.** Use a ribbon, bookmark, or sticky note to pause and resume with ease.

2) **Make it personal.** Keep a journal nearby to record your thoughts, prayers, or insights as you journey through the vignettes. Let Paul's life and letters shape your own.

# Introduction
## Profiles from Paul
### *A Companion to Beyond Expectations*

*"In the first book, O Theophilus, I have dealt with all that Jesus began to do and teach…"* —Acts 1:1

With those words, Luke bridges the story of Jesus to the story of the Church. What Jesus began, the early church carried forward—through the Spirit, through the apostles, and through a man named Paul.

*Profiles from Paul* serves as a companion to *Beyond Expectations: The Kingdom No One Expected*. In that earlier volume, we journeyed with Jesus—through parables and proclamations, miracles and meals, His suffering and His triumph. We glimpsed a Kingdom unlike any other: born not of force, but of faith; built not by swords, but by sacrifice. Jesus, the Servant-King, turned expectations upside down.

Now, we follow one of His most unexpected followers. Saul of Tarsus—the zealous persecutor turned apostle—was chosen as "*a vessel of My name*" to carry the gospel to Gentiles, kings, and Israelites (Acts 9:15). Through Paul's letters and journeys, we witness how the gospel took root in cities, cultures, and communities. The Kingdom announced by Jesus was given shape, language, and structure by Paul.

This shift is not merely stylistic—it is theological. Jesus emphasized the "Kingdom of God" more than fifty times; He mentioned the "church" only a handful. Paul, by contrast, speaks of the "church" nearly one hundred times. What Jesus initiated in His teaching, Paul clarified in his theology. The Kingdom became incarnate in community.

This book explores Paul's life and thought through theological vignettes—brief, focused reflections drawn from his letters and ministry. Each entry brings context, Scripture, and application, helping readers discover not just Paul's doctrine, but his devotion. Not just his theology, but his tears.

The result is not a commentary or biography, but a *narrative theology*—an unfolding journey of how the Kingdom moved from a cross outside Jerusalem to congregations across the empire.

Paul was not the founder of Christianity. He was not its architect. He was a servant of Christ, compelled by grace, willing to suffer, teach, and lead so that others might know the truth that had seized him.

Just as Jesus taught in parables and Paul wrote in letters, this book uses vignettes to form windows into truth. Our hope is that these reflections—rooted in Scripture and refined by years of pastoral experience—will equip, inspire, and deepen your journey of faith.

Paul's story is not over.

It continues in us.

Let's walk the road with him.

# 1

# The Road to Damascus

*Acts 9:1–9; Acts 22:6–11; Acts 26:12–18*

The sun rose like any other over the road north from Jerusalem to Damascus. Saul of Tarsus, the zealot of Pharisees, strode with conviction. Armed with authority and inner fire, he wasn't merely defending tradition—he was extinguishing heresy. In his mind, the followers of Jesus were defiling the purity of the faith he loved.

So he went with letters. And with fury.

But then came a light.

It wasn't a burst of daylight. It was something else entirely—a radiance that swallowed the sun and dropped Saul to the ground. A presence. A voice. A question that pierced him to his core:
*"Saul, Saul, why are you persecuting Me?"*

This wasn't metaphor. This was glory—the same effulgence that transfigured Jesus on the mountain, the same force that some believe scorched His image into the burial shroud. The light that struck Paul was not of this world. It was the Light of heaven itself.

In that instant, Saul encountered a truth too vast for words. The voice wasn't merely speaking about Christians. It was Christ. And He was alive.

Saul had believed he was serving God. But the Living God now stood before him—in the person of Jesus. He wasn't protecting the faith; he was attacking its fulfillment.

Trembling, blind, undone, he could only ask:
*"Who are you, Lord?"*
And the answer came:

*"I am Jesus, whom you are persecuting."*

That was the breaking point.

But not the whole transformation.

The blinding light had stopped him in his tracks, but conversion would take time. For three days he sat in the house on Straight Street—blind, neither eating nor drinking. No fury. No certainties. Just silence and shadow. The man of letters had no words. The man of power had no strength.

Then came Ananias, a reluctant messenger of grace. He laid hands on Saul and called him **brother**. And the scales fell. Sight returned. But more than that, vision arrived.

And with it, a mission.

Paul's encounter with Christ on the Damascus Road is one of the most pivotal moments in Christian history. But it wasn't instantaneous. The dramatic confrontation was only the beginning of a slow unmaking and remaking. Saul didn't just repent of wrong deeds. He had to relinquish an entire framework of belief.

This encounter underscores a truth central to Paul's theology: salvation is entirely by grace. Paul brought nothing to the table. He was not seeking Jesus; Jesus found him. His conversion reveals the initiative of divine grace, the cost of truth, and the power of mercy.

Sometimes we think of conversion as a moment. But often, it is a season. What began in blinding light for Paul continued in silence and submission. The same may be true for us.

Are there moments when God has stopped you in your tracks? Are there truths that took time for you to see clearly?

Paul's story reminds us that disorientation is often the first sign of transformation. And when we encounter the risen Christ, nothing remains the same.

### "The Light That Shattered Saul"

He walked in fire, he breathed the law,
With fury clothed and zeal for awe.
But on the road, the sky turned flame,
And heaven called him out by name.
"Why strike at Me with bitter breath?
Why cast My body into death?"
He knelt in dust with blinded sight,
Undone before the face of Light.
Three days of dark, three days alone,
Until grace spoke in gentler tone.
A hand was laid, a word was said—
And scales like pride fell where they bled.
Now vision came—not just to see,
But glimpse the truth that sets men free.
No longer Saul, with cause and sword,
But Paul, a servant of the Lord.


### Reflections from the Road

1. Has God ever stopped you on a path you were sure was right?

2. What role has silence or waiting played in your spiritual journey?

3. How does Paul's story help you understand grace as God's initiative—not our achievement?

4. Have you ever experienced transformation that took longer than expected—but proved deeper than imagined?

5. What is God calling you toward today, now that the Light has found you?

# 2

# Kicking Against the Goads
### *Acts 26:14; Acts 9:1–5; Philippians 3:4–8*

Before the blinding light, before the voice from heaven, before the road to Damascus turned into a road of no return, there was resistance. Saul of Tarsus had been kicking against the goads.

Jesus named it explicitly in His confrontation: "*It is hard for you to kick against the goads.*"

Goads are instruments of mercy wrapped in pain. A farmer used them to steer oxen on the right path, jabbing to prevent a wrong turn or dangerous delay. Saul's entire religious life was ordered, clean, impressive. But inside, his conscience was bleeding. And with every encounter—Stephen's radiant face, the courageous joy of Christians he imprisoned, the disconnect between his zeal and the peace he lacked—the goads pressed deeper.

His was not the hatred of the ignorant, but the fury of a man trying to silence the truth cracking through his own armor.

He had everything: birthright, education, credentials. He said so himself in Philippians 3. But when Jesus found him, Saul realized the staggering truth: All he had built was a pile of refuse next to the surpassing worth of knowing Christ.

The Damascus Road didn't mark the beginning of God's pursuit. It was the moment Saul stopped running. And the God who had been wounding was now ready to heal.

## "The Goad"

Not all pain is punishment,
Not all wounds are wrath.
Some stings are from a Shepherd's staff
That redirects our path.

A piercing glance, a martyr's prayer,
A question left unspoken.
Each goad, a whisper from the Lord:
Your heart is not yet broken.

He strikes to save, He wounds to win,
He shouts through deaf despair.
And when the fight is finally lost,
We fall—and find Him there.


## Reflections from the Road

1. Have you ever resisted a truth you knew deep down was from God? What were the "goads" that finally got your attention?

2. Why do you think Jesus mentioned the goads when He confronted Paul? What does that reveal about His approach?

3. How can you recognize the difference between God's correction and condemnation?

4. In what ways might God be using discomfort to draw you into a deeper relationship with Him?

5. Saul was transformed not just by truth, but by surrender. What might full surrender look like for you today?

# 3

# A Prepared Man for a Prepared Plan

## *Philippians 3:4–11; Acts 9:10–16; Acts 16:35–40*

Paul didn't arrive on the gospel stage unannounced. He was a man in motion long before the light stopped him cold outside Damascus. Trained under Gamaliel, fluent in the Law and the languages of empire, Paul was the sum of Jewish pedigree and Roman privilege. He was not merely educated—he was engineered for influence. Yet, in his own words, he would later count it all as loss. Everything that seemed to place him ahead of others only served to reveal how far behind he truly was.

The turning point wasn't a theological lecture or persuasive sermon. It was a Person. A light. A voice. "*Saul, Saul, why do you persecute Me?*" The collision of Paul's ambition with Christ's presence shattered every category he had. In persecuting the followers of the Way, he had struck at Jesus Himself. The persecutor became the pursued.

But the blinding flash wasn't the end—it was the beginning. In a humble home on Straight Street, clarity came. Not just physical sight, but spiritual vision. God told Ananias, "*He is a chosen instrument of mine.*" The irony was thick—Paul, the man who would one day argue that God shows no favoritism, was God's chosen vessel. Not for privilege, but for purpose. Not for power, but for proclamation. Paul would suffer for the sake of the name he once sought to destroy.

Years later, in a prison cell, Paul would again wield another unlikely piece of his past—his Roman citizenship. Beaten and imprisoned without trial, he refused to be released quietly. His citizenship was not a boast; it was a lever. A gospel opportunity. God had not wasted Paul's background—He had redeemed it. Even the law that once defined Paul became a tool in the advance of grace.

Paul's story is not about a man who found God, but about a God who prepared a man. Every thread—Jewish tradition, Greco-Roman intellect, legal privilege, and fervent zeal—was woven into a tapestry of redemption. Paul was not the center of the story. Jesus was. But Paul's life stands as a testimony to the God who shapes history through surrendered lives.


## "A Vessel, Shaped"

Clay spun beneath the Potter's hand,
A Pharisee, with future planned.
Zeal and law, his early name,
Till mercy lit a brighter flame.
He knew the scrolls, he knew the law,
But not the voice that stilled with awe.
On Straight Street, truth would claim his sight—
And blind no more, he walked in light.
Not cast aside, but wholly turned,
His pedigree as fuel now burned.
A Roman, Jew, and bondman too—
For Christ, he bore what few would do.
Prepared in flesh, refined by grace,
He ran the course, he kept the pace.
A vessel, shaped for God's design—
A servant of the Christ divine.


## Reflections from the Road

1. What past strengths, experiences, or even wounds might God be preparing to redeem for His purpose?

2. How has your background—education, upbringing, citizenship—shaped you for Kingdom use in ways you didn't expect?

3. What personal achievements or qualifications have you had to "count as loss" in order to follow Christ more fully?

4. Where might your story become someone else's path to grace?

5. What would it mean for you to live as a chosen instrument—humbly available and strategically placed by God?

# 4

# The Wilderness Between the Lines
### *Galatians 1:15–18; Acts 9:19–22*

Following Paul's dramatic conversion on the road to Damascus, Acts tells us he immediately began proclaiming Jesus as the Son of God. But between verses 21 and 22 in Acts 9 lies a quiet gap—three unspoken years spent in Arabia, mentioned only in Galatians 1. The timeline skips forward, but Paul disappears from the stage… only to reappear transformed. The difference was the wilderness between the lines.

Why Arabia?

It was not for rest. It was for reorientation.

Paul had spent a lifetime at the top of the religious hierarchy. A Hebrew of Hebrews. A Pharisee of precision. A zealot who once saw persecution as purity. But the blinding light of Christ cracked everything he thought he knew. The man who was sure of everything had to retreat, to unlearn—and to be taught afresh.

He didn't go to Jerusalem to seek apostolic validation. He wasn't asking Peter's permission. Paul went to the wilderness to be re-formed. The pattern is not new: Moses fled to the wilderness before returning to Egypt. Elijah heard God not in the wind, fire, or quake—but in the whisper of solitude. Jesus, after His baptism, was led into the wilderness to fast, to be tested, to be clarified.

So too, Paul.

He likely wrestled in that desert—re-reading Scripture in the light of Christ. Genesis to Malachi now glowed with new meaning. Salvation wasn't through law, but by faith—just like Abraham. Messiah wasn't a political liberator, but a crucified redeemer. The Gentiles were not intruders—they were heirs. Paul would later say, "I received [the gospel] by revelation from Jesus Christ." Arabia was not sabbatical. It was seminary.

Most readers miss the time gap. Acts reads quickly—but it spans decades. From chapter 9 to chapter 28, thirty years unfold. Paul's retreat to Arabia reminds us that spiritual growth is not microwave discipleship. Even for apostles, time away is essential.

What emerged from Arabia was not the same man. Acts 9:22 says, "But Saul grew more and more powerful and baffled the Jews in Damascus by proving that Jesus is the Messiah." The difference between verses 21 and 22 is the desert. Three hidden years. Silence that reshaped his soul.

In a world addicted to speed, retreat feels foreign. But what if some of our greatest transformation requires withdrawal? Not to abandon the world, but to see it anew. To hear again. To realign. Author Elton Trueblood once said that every believer should retreat twice a year—for perspective, not escape. Paul's retreat wasn't optional. Neither is ours. The world will wait. Your soul needs the silence.

## "Between the Lines"

A man once sure of every line,
Now stumbled blind where stars don't shine.
From law and zeal to desert sand,
He fell, then found the Potter's hand.
Not Rome, not ranks, not priestly fame—
But whispers spoke the Savior's name.
Three silent years, no stage, no crowd—
Just grace reshaping heart and vow.
The world would see his might unfold,
But not the forge where fire took hold.
Between the lines, in desert deep—
The truth would burn, the lies would sleep.


## Reflections from the Road

1. Have you ever experienced a time of retreat or disorientation that God used to reshape your understanding?

2. What lessons might God be teaching you "between the lines" right now?

3. What truths have become clearer in seasons of silence or solitude?

4. Could you schedule a personal retreat—however brief—to listen and realign your spirit?

5. How might your time in the wilderness become part of someone else's awakening?

# 5

# The Great Escape

*Acts 9:20–25; 2 Corinthians 11:32–33*

The desert had changed him. Arabia had stripped away the old certainties of Saul the Pharisee and begun to shape Paul the Apostle. And now, back in Damascus, the fire of that transformation could not be hidden.

He entered the synagogues not with timid caution, but with boldness—proclaiming that Jesus *is* the Son of God. The same man who once hunted believers now defended their Messiah with unmatched clarity and conviction. His arguments confounded the Jews in Damascus. The logic of Scripture, once his weapon against the Way, now testified to its truth. But clarity does not always win converts. Sometimes it hardens hearts.

As the days passed, opposition swelled. Whispers became threats. A plot emerged. The gates were watched. Paul's death was sought. The man who had once carried letters of authority now found himself a hunted man, his life hinging on secrecy and the kindness of disciples.

And so, in the night, they lowered him from a window in the city wall—hidden in a basket, silent, vulnerable, lowered by ropes into darkness.

It was not the heroic image of a great apostle. It was not triumphal. But it was telling.

The pattern of Paul's ministry was already being set: bold proclamation, fierce opposition, and divine preservation through unexpected means. He would spend the rest of his life fleeing mobs, appealing to governors, surviving shipwrecks, and enduring prisons—not as a victim, but as a witness. And this first escape, humbling and hidden, was a fitting beginning for a man who would later write, *"When I am weak, then I am strong."*

## The Reversal of Fortune

Paul's journey is a striking reversal. He arrived in Damascus as a man of power, status, and certainty. He had the full weight of Jerusalem's religious establishment behind him. He came as the hunter.

But God overturned his mission—and his identity. Paul left Damascus under cover of night, lowered over the wall in a basket like contraband. He was no longer feared; he was despised. No longer the instrument of authority, he became the object of suspicion and scorn. The hunter became the hunted.

This was not failure. It was formation.

In this moment, we glimpse a truth too often lost in modern Western Christianity: the call to follow Jesus is not a promise of ease, wealth, or comfort. It is a call to die. Jesus said, *"If the world hates you, keep in mind that it hated me first"* (John 15:18). Paul himself would later say, *"Everyone who wants to live a godly life in Christ Jesus will be persecuted"* (2 Tim. 3:12), and again, *"It has been granted to you on behalf of Christ not only to believe in him, but also to suffer for him"* (Phil. 1:29).

This humbling escape through the wall in Damascus stands in quiet defiance of the prosperity gospel. It reminds us that obedience may cost us everything—and that the presence of hardship is not the absence of God's favor but often the sign of it. Paul's "great escape" was not a defeat—it was a consecration.

## "Lowered in the Night"

He came with fire and fury armed,
With writs and threats in hand,
To root the followers of the Way
And purge them from the land.

But grace had knocked him to the dust,
And fire became a flame
That now declared with trembling lips
The glory of Christ's name.

He preached with power, heart aflame—
And faced the seething crowd,
Their anger rising with each word
That once would make him proud.

Now hunted by the ones he served,
Rejected by his kin,
He fled the walls of privilege
To find his strength within.

No sword, no steed, no shouting guard—
No honor to defend.
Just ropes, a wall, a basket's sway,
And silence without end.

But Heaven saw, and angels leaned,
And glory watched him fall,
For he who once had scaled in pride
Was lowered by the call.


## Reflections from the Road

1. What does Paul's escape from Damascus teach us about the cost
of true discipleship?

2. How does this vignette challenge the modern idea that blessing equals comfort and success?

3. When have you felt "lowered" by your obedience to Christ? How did God meet you there?

4. In what ways can suffering be a form of confirmation that we are on the right path?

5. How can we encourage others in our community who are experiencing hardship for their faith?

# 6

# The Return to Jerusalem

## *Acts 9:26–30; Galatians 1:18–24*

He had been gone for years.

The last time the church in Jerusalem had seen him, he was their enemy—the man who held the coats while Stephen was stoned, the man whose very name brought dread. *Saul of Tarsus* had been the terror of the early church. And then he disappeared.

Now, three or maybe four years later, he returned.

But everything had changed.

He came not in power but in peace. He came not to bind disciples but to become one. His face, lined now by solitude and the strain of persecution, bore no threat—but the believers could not forget. Time may heal wounds, but it doesn't always erase fear. When Saul tried to join them, they held back. They couldn't risk it. Not again.

Enter Barnabas.

They called him the *"Son of Encouragement."* A Levite from Cyprus, he had once sold his land and given the full proceeds to the apostles—an act of pure generosity in a community straining under the weight of explosive growth and dwindling resources. He had earned their trust. Now he gave that trust to Saul.

Barnabas stood with him. He took Paul to the apostles and vouched for his transformation—how he had seen the risen Lord, how he had preached boldly in Damascus, how his old fire had been repurposed for Christ. It was Barnabas who opened the door.

But the path wasn't easy. In Jerusalem, Paul found the same reaction he'd faced in Damascus: fierce resistance. He spoke freely, boldly—especially among the Hellenistic Jews—but the clarity of his message incited rage. The hunter was now the hunted once again.

And so, for his safety and theirs, the believers sent him away. Back to Tarsus. Back to obscurity. It was a quiet exit from the city where the apostles still held court. Paul had wanted to join the mission—but God had more preparation in store. Ten years more, in fact.

This, too, was part of the calling.

## When God Sends You Away

The story of Paul's return to Jerusalem is layered with tension and grace. It reveals the lingering wounds of persecution and the long shadow of a painful past. Conversion does not erase memory. Trust, especially among the wounded, takes time.

Paul may have imagined that his return to Jerusalem would be triumphant—that he would be welcomed as a trophy of grace. Instead, he was met with suspicion, silence, and then, violence.

But here we also meet Barnabas—one of the earliest examples of a spiritual bridge-builder. He risked his own credibility to lift Paul from the margins and bring him into fellowship. His act of encouragement reshaped Paul's path. Without Barnabas, Paul might have remained isolated. God often works through the faith of someone else to open the doors we cannot open for ourselves.

Yet even with Barnabas' support, Paul's boldness stirred up enemies—and the church made the hard decision to send him home. To Tarsus. To waiting.

This is not the chapter we expect from a man called to change the world. But it is a chapter we must learn to recognize. Sometimes God sends us away—not as punishment, but as preparation. The call remains, but the timing belongs to Him.

There is no prosperity gospel here—only a gospel of perseverance, patience, and purpose.

## "Sent Away"

He came with hope, with fire in hand,
To walk where saints had bled—
But doors stayed shut, eyes looked down,
And silence met his tread.

The ones he once had hunted long
Now shrank back from his name,
Their memories still raw with loss,
Their hearts unsure he'd changed.

Then came one whose name meant grace,
Who dared to stand and see—
Who risked his voice to lift a friend
And change his destiny.

But truth still stung, and fear ran deep,
And threats once more arose.
No triumph crowned his visit here—
Just danger, then repose.

And so he left, not by choice,
But by the church's will.
Not cast aside, but placed in wait,
While Heaven whispered: *Still.*

## Reflections from the Road

1. Why do you think the early church struggled to accept Paul, even after years had passed?

2. How does Barnabas' example challenge you to be an advocate or encourager for others?

3. Have you ever experienced a "Tarsus" season—where God removed you from activity for a time of waiting or preparation?

4. What can we learn about spiritual calling from the fact that Paul was sent away rather than sent forth?

5. How can we resist the temptation to equate rejection or delay with failure in our walk with Christ?

# 7

# The Call Comes Again

## *Acts 8:1–3; 8:26–40; 11:19–26*

The scattering began with blood.

The stones that crushed Stephen's life sent shockwaves through the young church in Jerusalem. Saul of Tarsus stood approvingly over the carnage—and in the days that followed, he led the charge to destroy the Way. Houses were raided, families torn apart, believers dragged into prison. It seemed like the end.

But God was just beginning.

Those who fled Jerusalem carried more than fear—they carried the gospel. Philip, one of the Seven chosen to serve, found himself in Samaria, proclaiming Christ among those once despised as half-breeds. Miracles followed. Conversions multiplied. Even the apostles, cautious at first, could not deny that the Spirit was moving beyond Jerusalem.

Then came an even stranger command:
*Go south.*
*Leave the crowds.*
*Find the desert road.*

Philip obeyed—and there he met a solitary traveler: an Ethiopian eunuch, treasurer to Candace the queen. A man ritually excluded under Jewish law. A man who was searching the Scriptures—specifically Isaiah's vision of the suffering Servant. When Philip explained that Jesus was the fulfillment, the eunuch's heart leapt. His question pierced the air:
*"What hinders me?"*

Nothing.
The water was near.
Faith was full.
Barrier after barrier fell in the presence of the risen Christ.

The gospel was moving unhindered.

Years later, the ripple of that same persecution reached Antioch. Refugees from Cyprus and Cyrene—ordinary believers—proclaimed Jesus not only to Jews, but to Greeks. A new frontier opened. The church in Jerusalem, ever cautious, sent Barnabas to investigate.

They chose the right man.

Barnabas, the Encourager, saw not a threat but a harvest. The Spirit's fingerprints were everywhere. He threw himself into the work—but it was too large for one man. He needed help. And he remembered another man, once feared, once fierce—a man now waiting in obscurity.

Tarsus wasn't far.

And so Barnabas went knocking.

Ten years had passed since Saul had fled Jerusalem, hidden away, shaped by solitude and silence. But when Barnabas found him, Saul was ready. The time of waiting was over. The second call had come—and this time, the whole world would hear.


## The Gospel Moves Unhindered

From the desert road of Gaza to the cosmopolitan streets of Antioch, the story of Acts is the story of divine initiative. Human hesitation cannot halt the purposes of God. Prejudice, persecution, and fear cannot chain the Word.

The eunuch's cry— *"What hinders me?"* —echoes through the centuries.
The answer from Heaven is clear: *Nothing.*

The gospel is for every race, every land, every heart willing to believe.

And sometimes, God's greatest servants must wait years before the door opens. Saul of Tarsus had zeal and intellect in abundance—but God's timing is precise. The intervening decade was not wasted; it was preparation. At the right moment, the right voice—Barnabas' voice—called him forward.

When God moves, nothing can hinder.
Not stones. Not fear. Not time.

## "The Knock at the Door"

Ten years in shadow, ten years in sand,
Ten years with calloused heart and hand.
Ten years of wondering, praying, still—
Ten years of bending to God's will.

The crowds forgot. The voices died.
The dream grew thin. The fire, denied.
Yet faith endured in silent breath,
And life sprang stubborn out of death.

Then came a knock—a friend's sure call—
A knock that shattered Tarsus' wall.
A voice that summoned not in shame—
But with the whisper of his name.

Ten years to forge what zeal could not—
A servant ready, fire-taught.
One knock, one call, one open door—
And Paul was hidden no more.


## Reflections from the Road

1. How does Philip's desert obedience challenge our expectations about success and significance in ministry? One of the oldest expressions of the Christian church in the world is the Ethiopian Coptic Church. Is it possible that the Ethiopian Christians trace their spiritual lineage through a eunuch who heard the gospel because a man named Philip obeyed the strange, seemingly contradictory, command of God?

2. What barriers in your own heart or culture might hinder the spread of the gospel today?

3. How does the story of Saul's years in Tarsus encourage you about God's use of hidden seasons in life?

4. Barnabas recognized the potential in someone others had forgotten. Who might God be calling you to encourage?

5. Are you ready to respond when the "knock at the door" comes—whether in calling, opportunity, or ministry?

# 8

# Forged in Silence, Revealed in Antioch

## *Acts 11:25–26*

The knock on the door came from Barnabas, but it might as well have been the hand of God.

For ten years, Saul of Tarsus had waited. Hidden from the spotlight. Forgotten by the leaders of Jerusalem. Shaped by silence, Scripture, and the stubborn work of his hands. As he stitched tents by day, he stitched together the fragments of his faith—threading the promises of Moses, the cries of the prophets, and the laments of the psalms into a new tapestry centered on Christ.

God had not wasted the silence.
He had used it to forge a man for His purposes.

Now, the call had come.

Barnabas led Saul to Antioch—a city teeming with energy, culture, and spiritual hunger. Here, among Greeks and Jews alike, the gospel was taking root. The work was massive. The fields were white. And for an entire year, Saul and Barnabas poured themselves into the new believers.

They didn't just preach sermons.
They taught.
They wrestled through Scripture.
They unfolded the mystery of Christ—the Messiah not only for Israel, but for the nations.
They taught salvation by grace through faith, the unity of Jew and Gentile in the body of Christ, the death of the old man and the life of the new.

It was there, in Antioch, under Saul's passionate instruction and Barnabas' encouragement, that the followers of Jesus were first called **Christians**—little Christs. Not just a sect of Judaism anymore. Something new had been born.

The forge of Arabia and Tarsus had done its work. The hammer blows of solitude, misunderstanding, and waiting had shaped a vessel strong enough to carry the gospel across empires.

And now the world was beginning to take notice.


## Forged for the Fire

Paul's theology was not born in the councils of Jerusalem.
It was hammered out in the lonely deserts and dusty workshops of his exile.

God forged him in silence—where the applause of men could not reach him, and the praise of Pharisees could no longer tempt him. In the long years of obscurity, Paul wrestled through every promise of the Hebrew Scriptures until Christ stood at the center of it all.

When Barnabas brought him to Antioch, he was ready.
Not polished. Not privileged.
But prepared.

And through his teaching, a movement was named. The world saw Christ reflected in His followers—and gave them His name.

The hammer blows of suffering had shaped more than a man.
They had shaped a message.

## "Hammered for Glory"

In desert hush, in workshop gloom,
Where dreams lay stitched beside the loom,
A man once fierce was tempered thin,
His roaring zeal burned clean within.

No crowd to cheer, no pulpit grand,
Just calloused thought and work-worn hand.
Yet in the silence, truth was mined,
And faith by fire was refined.

Then came the knock—the open door,
The forge gave way to something more.
The sparks that flew in lonely night
Now lit a world with Gospel light.

Forged by years no eye could see,
Hammered for Christ's victory.

## Reflections from the Road

1. Why is it significant that God prepared Saul in obscurity before using him publicly?
2. How do you think Saul's years of study and struggle shaped the gospel message he would later preach?
3. What does it say about God's timing that a man hidden for a decade became one of the most influential Christians in history?
4. When have you experienced a season of "silent forging" in your own life? What was God preparing you for?
5. How can we cultivate faithfulness and readiness during our own times of waiting?

# 9

## Called—*Apostolos*

### *Acts 11:27–30; 13:1–3*

The generosity of Antioch was already known.

When famine threatened the brothers in Judea, the church responded without hesitation. They gathered an offering—sacrificial, voluntary—and sent it by trusted hands. They chose Barnabas and Saul.

At that time, Barnabas was still the leading figure. His name came first. His character had already shaped Antioch's life: gracious, encouraging, open to the Spirit's unexpected movements. Saul was his partner, a powerful teacher still gaining trust among the churches. They journeyed to Jerusalem not as masters, but as servants—delivering the gift of love from Gentile believers to their Jewish kin.

When they returned, Antioch's fire had only grown brighter.

There were prophets and teachers now—voices tuned to the Spirit, hands devoted to the ministry of the Word. And while they worshiped, while they fasted—not striving, but waiting—the Holy Spirit spoke:

*"Set apart for Me Barnabas and Saul for the work to which I have called them."*

Not self-appointed.
Not elected by popularity.
Not structured by human hierarchy.
But **called**—recognized by the Spirit through the discerning worship of the gathered Body.

The church obeyed. They fasted again. They prayed. They laid

36

hands on Barnabas and Saul—not to confer authority as if it were theirs to give, but to affirm what Heaven had already decreed. Then they sent them forth—not with a pat on the back and good wishes, but with real provision, standing behind them with prayer, resources, and faith.

Thus began the first missionary journey—not the birth of professional clergy, but the unleashing of Spirit-gifted servants.

*Apostolos*—one sent with a commission.

The call to mission flowed not from ambition but from affirmation; not from human structures, but from divine sending.

## The Call Recognized

In the early church, the call of God was not a private experience detached from the community.

It was recognized, affirmed, and celebrated by the gathered Body.

Calling is often revealed through **gifting**—a natural and supernatural evidence of God's hand at work. Others see it, feel it, respond to it. In Antioch, the leaders and members discerned the Spirit's voice together, and they released their best—Barnabas and Saul—for the sake of the gospel.

There was no division between clergy and laity.
There was no professional priesthood.
There was only the *laos*—the people of God, moving in giftedness and obedience.

The laying on of hands was not an ecclesiastical ceremony.
It was an act of **recognition, affirmation**, and **sending**.

In Antioch, the forge of calling and community blazed bright. And when the Spirit spoke, they obeyed without fear or selfishness—even though it cost them their best leaders.

## "Set Apart"

Amid the songs, amid the fast,
Amid the prayers that rose and passed,
The Spirit spoke, the moment came,
And whispered each beloved name.

Not for pride, nor throne, nor fame,
Not called to gather wealth or name—
But set apart by Heaven's hand,
To sow the Word in foreign lands.

The hands laid on, the prayers arose,
The tears fell quiet as they chose
To send their best, to give their gold,
To trust the call, to loose the hold.

Set apart—not cast away—
But sent in love, to light the way.


## Reflections from the Road

1. Why is it important that Barnabas and Saul were called by the Spirit and affirmed by the congregation, not self-appointed?

2. How can the recognition of spiritual gifts by others help clarify our own sense of calling?

3. What does the Antioch church's willingness to send their best leaders teach us about generosity in mission?

4. How does the Spirit-led model of leadership differ from the clergy/laity structures that developed later in church history?

5. What gifts or callings might God be affirming in your life through the observations and encouragements of others?

# 10

# To the Synagogue First

*Acts 13:4–12*

When the Spirit called, the church sent.

Barnabas and Saul, newly commissioned by the believers in Antioch, set sail for Cyprus—Barnabas's homeland. John Mark went with them as their helper. And when they landed at Salamis, their first stop was deliberate: **to the synagogue first.**

This was no random choice. It was strategy—but more than strategy, it was sensitivity. The synagogue was the spiritual heart of every Jewish community. It contained the Scriptures. It nurtured expectancy. And around its periphery gathered Gentile God-fearers—souls hungry for something more.

Paul didn't see blank slates. He saw soil already turned. The people gathered there weren't strangers to God—they were straining toward Him. And Paul knew what the prophets had promised: that the Messiah had come. Now he would proclaim that Jesus of Nazareth was the One they had been waiting for.

From Salamis they journeyed across the island to Paphos. There, a Roman official named Sergius Paulus asked to hear the Word. But opposition flared. A Jewish sorcerer named Elymas tried to block the message. Paul, filled with the Spirit, rebuked him—and Elymas was struck blind. A judgment, but also an echo of Paul's own story. The one who had once tried to silence the gospel had been silenced himself. The proconsul believed.

The pattern was set: the Word to the synagogue, resistance from within, and openness from Gentiles. Paul's mission had begun.

## Grafted into Familiar Soil

Paul's gospel was radical—but he planted it carefully.

He didn't discard the old; he fulfilled it. Beginning in the synagogue showed both reverence for the past and hope for the future. Paul understood that gospel work often begins where God has already been at work.

The early church didn't copy the grandeur of the temple or the hierarchy of Rome. It mirrored the synagogue: local, participatory, elder-led, rooted in the Scriptures. These were not organizations built on charisma—they were communities built on calling, giftedness, and shared responsibility.

Paul appointed elders. Deacons served. Pastors taught and shepherded. And all were accountable to the Head—Christ. The church was meant to grow by equipping every member, not by exalting a few.

But drift was always a danger.

Even in the earliest churches, Paul warned of wolves in leadership, of structures becoming idols, of truth being twisted. His model remained clear: humble leaders, servant-hearted teams, Spirit-empowered community.


## "The First Step Forward"
In city streets where idols burned,
He walked the path the prophets turned—
To synagogues with sacred flame,
And scrolls that whispered Jesus' name.
Among the seats the seekers shared,
Prayers rose up like hopes laid bare,
He sowed the Word where hearts had tilled,
Where hope was old, but yet unfilled.
Then on to court where power reigned,

And sorcery the truth profaned—
One blinded heart met blindness true,
And saw the gospel's piercing view.
From island shore to pagan throne,
The Word went forth, the winds were blown.
Not with force, nor priestly gate,
But Spirit's fire and heaven's weight.


**Reflections from the Road**

1. What does Paul's synagogue-first strategy teach us about honoring spiritual heritage while proclaiming something new?

2. How does the early church's simple, Spirit-led structure challenge modern church models built on hierarchy and complexity?

3. What role did community familiarity (Scripture, shared expectation) play in how Paul approached new mission fields?

4. In what ways can "structure become supremacy" in today's churches, and how can we guard against that drift?

5. Have you ever found yourself standing in the tension between tradition and transformation? How did you navigate it?

# 11

# The Long Reach of Promise
## *Acts 13:13–41*

The journey pressed inland.

From the island of Cyprus, Paul and Barnabas sailed north to the southern coast of modern-day Turkey. They landed at Perga in Pamphylia—a difficult and disease-prone region. There, John Mark turned back. Whether from fear, illness, or something else, Scripture doesn't say. But the loss marked a shift in the team—and would surface again in future conflict.

Pressing onward, Paul and Barnabas climbed into the rugged highlands and arrived in Pisidian Antioch, a Roman colony nestled in the mountains. On the Sabbath, they entered the synagogue, and when the leaders offered Paul a chance to speak, he stood.

What followed was no casual homily. It was a masterpiece of biblical theology—a sweeping sermon that bridged the wilderness wanderings of Israel to the risen Christ. Paul told their story—Egypt, Canaan, judges, Samuel, kings. He focused on David, a man after God's heart, and from David's line, Paul proclaimed, came Jesus.

But Paul did not spiritualize Him.

Jesus was real. Born of a lineage. Living a real life. Dying a real death. Buried in a real tomb. And then—raised by God in real power (Romans 1:4).

Paul declared,

*"Therefore, my brothers, I want you to know that through Jesus the forgiveness of sins is proclaimed to you... Justification that the Law of Moses could never provide (Acts 13:38–39)."*

This wasn't abstraction. It was flesh and history. The God who promised had fulfilled His word in time, in space, in blood.

## A Faith Rooted in Flesh

Paul's sermon reminds us that Christianity is not grounded in myth or metaphor, but in a man—Jesus of Nazareth.

The early church marveled that such a man could be divine. Today, we reverse the tension: we affirm His deity easily, but struggle to grasp His full humanity.

But it is His full humanity that gives the gospel its shape and weight.

He walked dusty roads. He wept over friends. He bled under lashes. He was buried in a tomb. The resurrection was not a metaphor—it was a body raised, scarred and glorified.

Paul didn't proclaim a philosophy. He proclaimed a person. And in that person, the long reach of God's promise had found its fulfillment.

## "The Long Reach"

From fathers' tents to royal thrones,
From desert cries to temple stones,
The promise pressed through broken years,
Through crowned defeats and bloodstained fears.
It bore the weight of exiled sighs,
Of prophets' wounds and martyrs' cries,
Until one night in David's line,
A child was born—God's clear design.
A man of dust, a man of breath,
Who tasted hunger, grief, and death.
Yet from the grave He rose, and then
He made the broken whole again.

The reach of promise, long and wide,
Finds all its hope at Jesus' side.

### Reflections from the Road

1. Why did Paul root his message in Israel's history when proclaiming Jesus?

2. How does understanding the full humanity of Jesus deepen our appreciation for His suffering and resurrection?

3. What does Paul's sermon reveal about the early Christian message?

4. How does the historical reality of Jesus' life and resurrection strengthen your trust in the gospel?

5. What happens when we over-spiritualize Jesus and forget the grit of His incarnation?

# 12

# The Crown Without a Throne

## *Acts 14:8–20*

The miracle came quickly—and so did the confusion.

In the city of Lystra, Paul healed a man crippled from birth. The crowd, steeped in local legends, erupted in frenzy. They shouted in the Lycaonian language, declaring that the gods had come down among them.

They called Barnabas "Zeus"—Jupiter, the king of the gods. They called Paul "Hermes"—Mercury, the messenger and voice of the divine.

The priest of Zeus brought oxen and garlands to offer sacrifice before them.

It was a moment of deadly misunderstanding.

Paul and Barnabas tore their clothes in anguish, rushing into the crowd, pleading for reason:
*"We are men, just like you,"* Paul cried. *"We bring you good news, that you should turn from these worthless things to the living God."*

But the fevered adulation quickly soured.

Some Jews from Antioch and Iconium stirred the crowd to violence. The same voices that once hailed them as gods now turned to stone them.

Paul was dragged out of the city.
Bruised, battered, broken—left for dead on the Lystra rubbish heap.

No golden carriage.
No jeweled crown.
No sanctuary of marble or silk.

Just a battered body, a rejected message, and the hidden power of a Kingdom not of this world.


## The True Mark of Ministry

In Lystra, Paul wore the true marks of apostleship:

- Not wealth, but wounds.
- Not acclaim, but rejection.
- Not power over others, but love poured out for others.

The early church knew nothing of palace gates, golden chalices, or jeweled miters.

They followed a Savior who had nowhere to lay His head, and apostles who often had nowhere safe to stand.

The Kingdom of God advances not by spectacle, but by sacrifice. Not by dominance, but by dying daily.

Paul's near-death in Lystra is a searing reminder:
The crown of Christ is a cross before it is a glory.
The throne of Christ was first a tree.

And those who would bear His name must walk His road.

### "The Crown Without a Throne"
The crippled danced, the crowd went wild,
They crowned the men, they brought the child,
The oxen, garlands, songs, and cries—
Mistook the gift for gods disguised.

But truth spoke plain, and fury rose—
The hands that blessed now threw the stones.
The crowned was crushed, the king was slain—
Yet rose again to preach again.

No gilded hall, no throne of might,
Just battered hands and fearless light.
The true crown shines not made of gold,
But in a life poured out, made bold.

### Reflections from the Road

1. Why do you think the crowd so quickly shifted from worshiping Paul and Barnabas to trying to kill them?

2. How does Paul's experience in Lystra challenge modern ideas of ministry success?

3. What dangers arise when Christian leaders seek power, wealth, or

status instead of the humility of Christ?

4. How can we recognize and celebrate faithful servants of Christ today, even if their lives do not fit the world's image of success?

5. What does it mean in your life to wear "the crown without a throne"?

## Final Thought

This story stands among the most important in Paul's journey—not only because it reveals what he endured, but because it reclaims the true vision of Christian ministry. In a world still tempted by spectacle and success, the Spirit calls us back to the shape of the cross. It's not polished gold; it's bloodied obedience.
It's not prestige; it's perseverance.
It's not conquest; it's cruciform love.

May we learn to wear the crown without the throne—and find joy in the footsteps of the crucified and risen King.

Thank you, Lord, for leading us to this moment. And preserving it for our edification.

# 13

# Elders, Not Executives

*Acts 14:21–28; Acts 20:17, 28; 1 Peter 5:1–4*

The journey had changed them.

Paul and Barnabas retraced their steps through the cities where wounds still throbbed and threats still simmered. Lystra. Iconium. Antioch of Pisidia. They returned not to make grand speeches or claim victories, but to strengthen the souls of the disciples and **appoint elders** in every congregation.

Their model was simple.
The Spirit called.
The Body affirmed.
The elders shepherded.

These were not executives.
Not distant rulers installed by foreign hierarchy.
Not career professionals seeking platforms or titles.

They were **local men**, recognized for their character, their faith, their giftedness to teach and guide.
They were **shepherds**—guardians of the flock entrusted to their care.

Paul's vocabulary reflected the Spirit's intent:

- *Presbuteros*—elder, the wise and spiritually mature.

- *Episkopos*—overseer, one who watches with care.

- *Poimen*—shepherd, one who tends, protects, and feeds.

Three words for one office.

Three angles on one calling.
Not a ladder to climb, but a burden to bear.

The early churches were structured, but simply.
They were **autonomous but spiritually united**—bound together not by rigid chains of control, but by shared faith, shared mission, and the shared Lordship of Christ.

When the work of strengthening and appointing was done, Paul and Barnabas made their way back to Antioch of Syria—the church that had first laid hands on them in hope and prayer.

They came **not to boast**, but to **report**.

*"When they had gathered the church together, they reported all that God had done with them and how He had opened a door of faith to the Gentiles"* (Acts 14:27).

Not what *they* had done. What **God** had done *with* them.

Their stewardship was complete:

- Souls had been saved.

- Churches had been planted.

- Elders had been set in place.

And Paul, perhaps weary in body but burning in spirit, **took up pen and parchment**. During this season of staying and strengthening, Paul would write his first epistle—*Galatians*—bearing the marks of his own hand, strained eyes, and a soul unwilling to leave the new believers undefended.

The mission was expanding. Spirit-led leadership and accountable mission were bearing fruit—in lives changed, churches strengthened, and a gospel taking root.

And the Kingdom was advancing—not with empire's banners, but with the shepherd's staff and the servant's heart.

## Servants, Not Celebrities

Paul's vision for church leadership stands in sharp relief against many modern models.

- Leaders were **identified, not manufactured**.

- Authority was **recognized, not assumed**.

- Churches were **strengthened, not franchised**.

The early Christians lived as a spiritual family, not a corporate empire.
Their leaders were **elders**, not executives.
Their accountability was **relational**, not institutional.

When leaders see themselves as stewards, not owners, the Body grows strong.
When churches see themselves as the people of God, not the property of personalities, the gospel flourishes.

The Spirit still calls.
The Body still affirms.
The mission still belongs to God.

Paul's leadership model speaks prophetically to our modern moment—not with condemnation, but with credibility. It is theologically grounded, historically anchored, and refreshingly free of pretense. His pastoral pattern invites us back to something deeper, something real.


## "The Shepherds Rose"

They laid no golden crown on heads,
No silken robes, no marble beds—
But calloused hands and prayer-worn eyes,
And hearts that heard the Spirit's cries.

Shepherds rose with steadfast zeal,
To guard the flock on dusty hills,
To watch, to feed, to mend, to weep,
And in their care, the Kingdom deep.

They claimed no throne, no priestly seat,
But walked the roads with broken feet,
And led by love, and taught by grace,
Until they saw their Shepherd's face.


## Reflections from the Road

1. What does Paul's pattern of elder appointment teach us about the simplicity and Spirit-led nature of early church leadership?

2. How does the modern church sometimes drift from the relational, pastoral model Paul and Barnabas embodied?

3. What does true spiritual stewardship look like—for leaders and for congregations?

4. How can we practice accountability and shared mission today without creating rigid hierarchies?

5. What might God be calling you to in terms of strengthening and shepherding others in your community?

# Interlude

# The Compass Before the Climb
### *A Pause Before Paul's Letters*

Paul didn't leave us a systematic theology.
He left us letters—beginning with Galatians.

Urgent, pastoral, passionate letters—written in the thick of spiritual warfare, moral confusion, ethnic tension, and explosive growth. These were not essays from a quiet study. They were dispatches from the front lines of the Kingdom.

And yet, woven through the individual moments—Galatia's legalism, Corinth's chaos, Thessalonica's fear—there is a unified voice. A gospel heartbeat.
A compass.

In *Galatians*, the earliest of his letters, Paul lit a fire: salvation by grace, not law…freedom in Christ, not bondage to the flesh…life in the Spirit, not mere religion. These ideas didn't stay in Galatia. They echo in *Romans*, where Paul builds his most expansive case for justification by faith. They rise again in *Ephesians*, where grace and unity form the cornerstone of the church's identity. They even whisper through *Corinthians*, where discipline is rooted not in legalism, but in love.

Paul's letters can be grouped by occasion—but their theology is braided. Themes recur, deepen, and expand:

- **Grace over Law** — The gospel begins and ends with what Christ has done, not what we must do.

- **Unity in the Body** — Jew and Gentile, slave and free, rich and poor—one new humanity in Christ.

- **Spiritual Formation** — Christ formed in you. Not just belief, but character.

- **Leadership and Order** — Pastors and deacons. Elders and overseers. Paul laid down blueprints still in use.

- **Endurance in Suffering** — Glory is coming. But for now: scars, shipwrecks, and a thorn in the flesh.

- **The Return of Christ** — Always near. Always shaping how we live today.

Each letter speaks to its moment. But together, they form a constellation—each star adding light to the gospel Paul received and passed on. His was the voice that explained Jesus to the Gentile world. His letters became the infrastructure of the early church.

Without Paul, the life of Jesus might have been a memory.
Because of Paul, it became a movement.

So as we now turn to *Galatia*, and eventually Corinth, Rome, Ephesus, Philippi, and beyond—let's listen not just for what Paul says to them, but for what the Spirit is still saying to us.

The terrain ahead will be rough at times. But we know the direction. Because we've seen the compass.

### "Ink and Fire"

He did not write from safety's side,
But from the battle's din—
With chains upon his weathered hands,
And gospel in his pen.
Each line a flame, each word a spark,
To scatter through the night—

A letter lit by prison's dark
To set the world alight.


**Reflections from the Road**

1. Which of Paul's recurring themes—grace, unity, endurance, transformation—speaks most to your current spiritual season?

2. How might viewing Paul's letters as a connected body of work change the way you read them?

3. Why do you think God chose to preserve these letters, written under pressure, as the backbone of New Testament theology?

4. What does Paul's example teach us about writing, leadership, and legacy in a time of crisis?

5. If you had to choose one "compass verse" from Paul's writings to guide your walk this year, what might it be?


# 14

# The Crisis in Galatia


It did not take long for trouble to find the young churches.

After Paul and Barnabas returned from their first missionary journey, news came back across the rugged hills of south Galatia—news that broke Paul's heart and ignited his pen.

False teachers had crept in.
Men bearing familiar words but empty hearts.
They did not deny Christ entirely—

But they added burdens Christ never laid:

- Circumcision,
- Law-keeping,
- Ritual performance.

They claimed that faith in Christ was good—but not enough.
They sought to drag the newborn Gentile believers back under the heavy yoke of the old covenant.
And in doing so, they risked distorting the gospel beyond recognition.

Paul could not, would not, stand by.

Galatians is his earliest surviving letter.
It was not written from a comfortable study.
It poured from a heart wounded by betrayal, burning with urgency, yet anchored in deep pastoral love.

### The Situation Behind the Letter

- **Who?** Paul—scarred by suffering, sharpened by grace, and utterly committed to the purity of the gospel he had received directly from Christ.

- **When?** Shortly after the first missionary journey (Acts 13–14), but **before** the Jerusalem Council of Acts 15.

- **Where?** Addressed to the churches of **south Galatia**—Lystra, Iconium, Derbe—the very cities where Paul had preached, bled, and nearly died.

- **Why?** To **defend the gospel of grace, protect Gentile believers** from legalistic captivity, and **proclaim again** the freedom found in Christ alone.

## A Letter Like Fire

Galatians is not a polite theological treatise.
It is a battlefield letter.

Paul does not begin with his usual words of thanksgiving.
He opens with astonishment—and warning:

*"I am astonished that you are so quickly deserting the one who called you to live in the grace of Christ and are turning to a different gospel."* (Galatians 1:6)

This is the tone of the whole letter:

- Urgent.

- Uncompromising.

- Yet full of pastoral longing for his spiritual children to return to the freedom they had first received.

Paul does not argue from cold authority.
He pleads from personal experience.
He reminds them that his calling, his gospel, and his ministry come **not from men, but from God Himself**.

In Galatians, the stakes are clear:
It is not a debate about minor doctrines.
It is a fight for the soul of the church.

If grace is lost, the cross is emptied.
If the law is added, freedom is forfeited.
If Christ is not enough, all is lost.


## "Letter of Fire"

No silver pen, no studied prose,
But fire where living waters flowed.
A heart once chained now fiercely free,

Cried out to guard Christ's liberty.

No second cross, no other yoke,
No law to bind what grace had broke.
Only the Savior, lifted high—
The cross alone, the reason why.

## Reflections from the Road

1. Why did Paul respond so urgently and forcefully to the situation in Galatia?

2. What are some ways the gospel of grace can still be distorted today by human additions?

3. How does knowing the personal cost Paul paid deepen your appreciation for the purity of his message?

4. Why is it important to guard not just the truth of the gospel, but the freedom it brings?

5. Where do you sense the Spirit calling you to stand firm in grace, even when others might compromise?

# 15

# No Other Gospel

## *Galatians 1:1–10*

The ink dried slowly under Paul's straining eyes.

This letter was not dictated through a scribe, polished and polished again.
It was poured out **in Paul's own hand**, rough with passion, fire, and grief.
It bore the weight of urgency—and the scars of love.

After returning to Antioch, after reporting the wonders God had done among the Gentiles, Paul heard troubling news.
The churches he and Barnabas had planted in Galatia—in Lystra, Iconium, Derbe—were faltering.
False teachers had crept in, men insisting that salvation required more than Christ—that Gentile believers must bear the yoke of the Jewish law to be fully part of God's people.

Paul was stunned.
And heartbroken.
And righteously angry.

*"I am astonished that you are so quickly deserting the one who called you to live in the grace of Christ and are turning to a different gospel"* (Galatians 1:6).

Galatians is Paul's **first letter**—the raw, unfiltered defense of the gospel he had lived, suffered, and nearly died for.
It is not a cool theological treatise; it is a rescue mission.

With sharp clarity, Paul reaffirms:

- Salvation is by **grace through faith** alone.

- The **law was a guardian**, not a savior.

- In Christ, a **new covenant** has come—not based on works, but on promise and Spirit.

- Gentiles are **full heirs** with Jews, not second-class citizens.

In every stroke of the pen, Paul fights for the freedom of the gospel and the full humanity of Christ.

Galatians is not a polite correction.
It is a battlefield letter.
A cry from a heart that refuses to let his spiritual children be enslaved again.

*"If anyone is preaching to you a gospel other than what you accepted, let them be under God's curse!"* (Galatians 1:9).

There is no other gospel.
And there is no other name under heaven by which we are saved.


## The Gospel at Stake

Paul's defense of grace in Galatians is fierce because the stakes are eternal.
If salvation depends on human effort, Christ died for nothing.
If righteousness comes by works, then the cross is emptied of its power.

Paul's fiery passion was born not of ego, but of a profound understanding:

- The cross of Christ fulfilled what the law only foreshadowed.

- The promises of Jeremiah 31—a new covenant written on hearts, not stone—had come true.

- To retreat into legalism was not just a mistake; it was a betrayal of the very grace that saved them.

Galatians stands at the crossroads of faith and flesh, Spirit and law, freedom and bondage.

And Paul's voice, carried across centuries, still calls:
*"Stand firm, then, and do not let yourselves be burdened again by a yoke of slavery."* (Galatians 5:1)

## "No Other Name"

No golden rule, no heavy chain,
No burden borne to earn His name.
No rite, no law, no shadowed deed—
But Christ alone for every need.

No race, no rank, no work, no worth,
Could buy the blood that claimed the earth.
No other way, no other flame—
Just grace, and faith, and Jesus' name.

## Reflections from the Road

1. Why was Paul so urgent and passionate in his letter to the Galatians?

2. How can we recognize modern forms of legalism that threaten to add to the gospel of grace?

3. Why is it crucial to understand salvation as entirely a work of God's grace, not our merit?

4. What does it mean to live daily in the freedom Christ has given?

5. Where do you feel called to defend or proclaim the "no other gospel" message today?

# 16

# Crucified with Christ

## *Galatians 2:16–21*

The lines were drawn early.

In Antioch, Paul had seen even the great Peter falter—stepping back from Gentile believers under pressure from Jerusalem's legalists. The gospel was at stake, and Paul knew it.

*"We are not justified by the works of the law,"* he said, *"but by faith in Jesus Christ."*

Not by circumcision.
Not by rituals.
Not by merit.
Only by grace through faith.

Paul's words in Galatians 2 rise like a clear trumpet call above the confusion of works-based religion.
He speaks not as a theorist, but as a man who had been crucified alongside his Lord in the deepest places of the soul.

*"I have been crucified with Christ and I no longer live, but Christ lives in me. The life I now live in the body, I live by faith in the Son of God, who loved me and gave Himself for me."* (Galatians 2:20)

This is no abstract theology.
It is **personal, visceral, transformative**.

To be justified—to be declared righteous before God—is not the achievement of moral effort.

It is the miracle of union: dying with Christ, rising with Christ, living by Christ.

The law could reveal sin.
The law could condemn sin.
But only the cross could kill it—and only the resurrection could give new life.

## Dead to Law, Alive to Grace

When Paul speaks of being crucified with Christ, he speaks of a death that already happened—
A death to self-reliance.
A death to the illusion of personal righteousness.
A death to the grinding, never-enough slavery of trying to earn God's favor.

The Christian life is not moral improvement.
It is a death and a resurrection.
It is Christ living His life through us, by faith, every day.

Anything less is a return to chains.

*"I do not set aside the grace of God,"* Paul says, *"for if righteousness could be gained through the law, Christ died for nothing!"* (Galatians 2:21)

The cross stands as both judgment and invitation:

- Judgment on all our vain efforts to save ourselves.

- Invitation to life by a new and living way.

## "Crucified with Christ"

Not patched or mended, not made new,
But buried deep, the old man through—
A cross, a grave, a finished breath,
A life now born from out of death.

No longer striving, gasping, chained,
No longer clothed in guilt and shame.
But Christ within, and Christ alone—
My hope, my heart, my cornerstone.


## Reflections from the Road

1. How does understanding "being crucified with Christ" change the way we think about Christian growth?

2. Why is justification by faith alone essential to the gospel?

3. What does it mean to truly live by faith day-to-day rather than by effort or self-reliance?

4. Where in your life are you tempted to "set aside the grace of God" and return to works-based thinking?

5. How does remembering the cross as a completed work strengthen your confidence and joy in Christ?

# 17

# The Promise Fulfilled

## *Galatians 3:6–29*

Abraham lived before there was a law to obey.

Before Sinai.
Before Moses.
Before commandments were etched in stone.

And yet Abraham was called **the friend of God**.
Not because of rule-keeping.
Not because of rituals.
But because of **faith**.

*"Abraham believed God, and it was credited to him as righteousness."* (Galatians 3:6)

When Paul faced the growing confusion in Galatia—voices urging the young believers to chain themselves to the law—he reached back, far beyond Moses, to the bedrock of the covenant itself.

The true children of Abraham were not marked by circumcision or works.
They were marked by faith—the same living trust that stirred Abraham to leave his home, to believe the impossible, to walk with God into unseen futures.

Faith was always the key.
Grace was always the plan.

The law, Paul said, came later—not to save, but to **guard**.
It was a tutor, a guidepost, a fence around a people waiting for the fullness of time.
But now that Christ had come, the guardian was no longer needed.

64

*"You are all sons of God through faith in Christ Jesus,"* Paul wrote. *"There is neither Jew nor Greek, slave nor free, male nor female, for you are all one in Christ Jesus.*
*If you belong to Christ, then you are Abraham's seed, and heirs according to the promise."* (Galatians 3:26–29)

The family of God was bigger than anyone had imagined.
And the inheritance was by promise, not by performance.


## Faith: The Ancient and Living Way

The story of salvation is not a new story.
It is as ancient as Abraham—and as alive as today.

The writer of Hebrews would later celebrate this legacy:

*"By faith Abraham, when called to go to a place he would later receive as his inheritance, obeyed and went, even though he did not know where he was going... For he was looking forward to the city with foundations, whose architect and builder is God."* (Hebrews 11:8–10)

Faith moves.
Faith trusts.
Faith waits for what only God can give.

The promise made to Abraham was fulfilled in Christ.
And through Christ, it extends to all who believe—no matter their background, their history, their standing in the eyes of men.

We are heirs of the promise because we are children of faith.
The law was a road marker.
But faith is the road home.

## "Heirs of the Promise"

Before the law, before the stone,
A heart believed, a grace was sown.
A whispered call, a desert sky,
A man who dared to walk, to try.

No tablets carved, no temple high,
Just trust that marked him friend and child.
And so we walk where Abram trod,
By faith alone, by grace of God.

No walls, no ranks, no walls remain,
The promise falls like gentle rain.
On all who trust, on all who dare—
We are His heirs. We are His heirs.


## Reflections from the Road

1. Why is Abraham such an important figure in understanding salvation by grace through faith?

2. How does Paul's view of the law as a temporary guardian help clarify its purpose in God's plan?

3. What does it mean for you personally to be an heir of God's promises by faith and not by works?

4. How can remembering Abraham's faith encourage you when God's promises feel distant or unseen?

5. In what ways does the unity described in Galatians 3:28 challenge the divisions often found in churches today?

# 18

## Adopted at the Right Time

### *Galatians 4:4–7*

Timing matters.

A whisper in the wrong season is lost.
A harvest too soon is wasted.
A promise fulfilled too late brings no joy.

But when God moves, the timing is perfect.
Not early. Not late.
At just the right moment.

*"But when the fullness of time had come, God sent His Son, born of a woman, born under the law, to redeem those under the law, that we might receive adoption to sonship."* (Galatians 4:4–5)

Across the centuries, the prophets had spoken of a day when the old would give way to the new.
Jeremiah saw it from afar:

*"The days are coming,"* declares the Lord,
*"when I will make a new covenant with the people of Israel and with the people of Judah...*
*I will put my law in their minds and write it on their hearts.*
*I will be their God, and they will be my people."* (Jer. 31:31–33)

No longer laws carved in stone.
No longer access gated by bloodlines and rituals.
A new covenant—written in Spirit and sealed in grace.

And when Christ came—at the *"fullness of time"*—He fulfilled what was promised.

The writer of Hebrews would later echo Paul's vision:

*"But now He has appeared once for all at the consummation of the ages to do away with sin by the sacrifice of Himself."* (Hebrews 9:26)

The time was full.
The covenant was ready.
The Son was sent.

Not simply to instruct or inspire, but to **redeem**.
To purchase freedom.
To adopt sons and daughters.
To place His Spirit into their hearts—the Spirit by whom we cry, *"Abba, Father."*

Adoption was not an afterthought.
It was the goal of redemption all along.


**The Fullness of Time, the Fullness of Grace**

God is never hurried.
Never delayed.
He orchestrates His promises with the patience of eternity and the precision of sovereignty.

At the moment Rome ruled the world,
When Greek language linked the continents,
When longing for Messiah burned in the hearts of a weary people—
The Christ came.

Born of a woman.
Born under the weight of the law.
Yet born to lift the weight once and for all.

Through His death, He fulfilled the covenant.
Through His resurrection, He inaugurated the Kingdom.

Through His Spirit, He sealed the adoption.

We are not servants grasping at God's door.
We are sons and daughters, welcomed at His table.

In Christ, the waiting is over.
The family is open.
The promise is fulfilled.


## "At the Fullness of Time"

Not early sent, nor late delayed,
But at the hour when hope had frayed—
The silence cracked, the heavens stirred,
And God enfleshed His final Word.

A cradle rocked where stars once burned,
A cry where angel songs returned.
The covenant carved not in stone,
But in a heart made flesh, His own.

And by His blood, the claim was sealed,
The orphaned heart by love was healed.
Adopted now, by cross and sign,
Sons and daughters, His and Mine.


## Reflections from the Road

1. What does the *"fullness of time"* reveal about God's sovereignty over history and salvation?

2. How does the promise of Jeremiah 31 connect to what Christ accomplished through the New Covenant?

3. What does adoption into God's family mean for your daily identity and security in Christ?

4. How does reflecting on the perfect timing of Christ's coming encourage you when waiting on God's promises in your own life?

5. In what ways can you live more fully as an adopted son or daughter of God, secure in His love and grace?

# 19

## Freedom's Fight

### *Galatians 5:1, 5:13–26*

The gospel brings freedom.
But freedom, if untended, can drift into chaos.
And chaos, if unguarded, becomes bondage all over again.

Paul saw the danger clearly.

*"It is for freedom that Christ has set us free. Stand firm, then, and do not let yourselves be burdened again by a yoke of slavery."* (Galatians 5:1)

Freedom is not an invitation to lawlessness.
It is a call to Spirit-led living.
It is a liberation from self-striving, not a license for self-serving.

*"You, my brothers and sisters, were called to be free. But do not use your freedom to indulge the flesh; rather, serve one another humbly in love."* (Galatians 5:13)

The Christian life is not a balancing act between law and license.
It is a **new way of life** altogether—powered by the Spirit, shaped by love, bearing fruit that cannot be manufactured by human effort.

Paul names the battleground with clarity:

- The **flesh** seeks self-gratification.

- The **Spirit** calls to self-giving love.

The works of the flesh are obvious—ugly fractures of relationship and soul: sexual immorality, hatred, jealousy, fits of rage, selfish ambition, and more.

But the fruit of the Spirit grows quietly, beautifully, where Christ reigns within:

*"Love, joy, peace, patience, kindness, goodness, faithfulness, gentleness, and self-control."* (Galatians 5:22–23)

Against such things, there is no law.
No need for enforcement, no need for compulsion.
Only life—free, full, flourishing.


## Freedom and the Spirit

Freedom is a gift.
But Spirit-formed character is a fight.
It requires walking daily, choosing constantly, surrendering repeatedly.

Paul doesn't promise an easy stroll.
He describes a **walk**—a deliberate, ongoing movement in step with the Spirit.

*"Since we live by the Spirit, let us keep in step with the Spirit."* (Galatians 5:25)

Freedom is not the absence of a master.
It is allegiance to the only Master who gives life instead of chains.

The fight for freedom is the fight for Spirit-filled living, day by day, choice by choice, surrender by surrender.

## "Freedom's Fight"

Not freedom loose, nor freedom wild,
But freedom born as Spirit's child—
Not license grasped with greedy hands,
But love poured out at His commands.

Not chains of law, nor lust's disguise,
But fruit that blooms where death once lied:
Love, joy, and peace in Spirit grown—
A harvest planted by His own.

So walk the road the Spirit paves,
And fight the fight that grace still saves.


## Reflections from the Road

1. How does Paul distinguish between true Christian freedom and the indulgence of the flesh?

2. Why is Spirit-led living described as a "walk" rather than a single decision?

3. In what ways do you experience the tension between the desires of the flesh and the desires of the Spirit?

4. Which fruit of the Spirit do you most long to see grow more fully in your life right now?

5. How can walking in the Spirit reshape not only your private life, but also your relationships and community?

# 20

# Glory Only in the Cross

## *Galatians 6:14–17*

Paul carried scars.

Not medals.
Not honors.
Not trophies.

Scars.

Each one told a story.
Each one whispered the true cost of faithfulness.

*"From now on, let no one cause me trouble, for I bear on my body the marks of Jesus."* (Galatians 6:17)

In a world obsessed with status and achievement, Paul's boast was stunning:

*"May I never boast except in the cross of our Lord Jesus Christ, through which the world has been crucified to me, and I to the world."* (Galatians 6:14)

The cross was not a symbol of prestige.
It was a sign of death, humiliation, and utter weakness.
And yet, it was the only thing Paul was willing to claim.

The cross was his identity.
The cross was his victory.
The cross was his glory.

Years later, writing to the Corinthians, Paul would echo the same heartbeat:

*"I resolved to know nothing while I was with you except Jesus Christ and Him crucified."* (1 Corinthians 2:2)

Not Christ the teacher.
Not Christ the healer.
Not Christ the revolutionary.

*Christ crucified!*

Paul understood what many still stumble to see:

- The cross: not the embarrassment of the gospel—it is its power.

- The cross: not the prelude to victory—it is the victory.

- The cross: not the shame of Christianity—it is its shining glory.

Through the cross, the world system—its ambitions, its vanities, its corrupt powers—was crucified.
Through the cross, Paul found freedom to die to that world and live wholly to God.

The cross stood at the center of his message, his mission, and his life.

## Boasting in the Right Place

In Galatia, as in every age, there were temptations to boast:

- In religious performance.

- In cultural heritage.

- In spiritual accomplishments.

But Paul had abandoned all those altars.
He boasted only in the one thing that canceled every claim of pride:
the shameful, beautiful, bloody cross.

To boast in the cross is to lay down all other crowns.

It is to see oneself not as a builder of empires, but as a follower of a crucified King.

It is to live crucified to the world's measures of success—and alive to Christ alone.

## "The Marks I Boast"

Not crowned with gold, nor robed in white,
But marked by scars of love's fierce fight—
The world's acclaim, I count as loss;
I boast alone in blood-stained cross.

No merit mine, no banner flown,
No wisdom save the Christ I've known.
The world behind, the cross before—
This scarred and sacred path I soar.

## Reflections from the Road

1. Why does Paul choose to boast only in the cross, rather than in spiritual achievements or religious heritage?

2. How does the cross both humble us and set us free?

3. In what ways does boasting in the cross reorient our identity and purpose?

4. What *marks of Jesus* are visible—or growing—in your life as you follow Him?

5. How might remembering the centrality of the cross transform the way you measure success and faithfulness?

# 21

# Jerusalem Council: Freedom Affirmed

## *Acts 15:1–35*

The city was crowded, tense.
The stakes could not have been higher.

In the shadow of the temple, where the old covenant rituals still echoed, the leaders of the early church gathered.
Paul and Barnabas came with stories from distant cities—stories of Gentile faith, Spirit-born and Spirit-sealed.
But not everyone rejoiced.

Some Jewish believers—zealous for their traditions—argued that Gentile converts must be circumcised and commanded to obey the Law of Moses.
Old loyalties die hard.

This was no minor debate.
At risk was the very heart of the gospel:

- Would salvation be by grace through faith alone?

- Or would it be grace *plus* works of the law?

- Would the church be a global people?

- Or merely a rebranded sect of Judaism?

Paul knew what was at stake.
His recent letter to the Galatians still burned in his mind and heart:
"*Did you receive the Spirit by the works of the law, or by believing what you heard?*" (Galatians 3:2)

He knew the answer.

He had seen the answer—among Gentiles in Lystra, Iconium, Derbe.
Faith, not circumcision.
Grace, not law.

Peter stood and spoke first:
*"God, who knows the heart, showed that He accepted them by giving the Holy Spirit to them, just as He did to us... We believe it is through the grace of our Lord Jesus that we are saved, just as they are."* (Acts 15:8,11)

Then James, the brother of Jesus, brought the final word—anchoring the council's decision not just in experience, but in prophecy:

*"The words of the prophets are in agreement with this... 'I have made you a light for the Gentiles, that you may bring salvation to the ends of the earth.'"* (Acts 13:47; cf. Isaiah 49:6)

The Council decided:

- No yoke of circumcision.

- No burden of the full Mosaic law.

- Only a few guidelines for unity and purity.

Freedom was affirmed.
Grace was preserved.
The gospel was safeguarded for all nations.

And in a beautiful, pastoral act, the council sent a **letter**—a hidden epistle—to the Gentile believers:
a word of encouragement, welcome, and relief.

*"It seemed good to the Holy Spirit and to us not to burden you with anything beyond the following requirements..."* (Acts 15:28)

The future of the church had turned on that day.
Not by sword, not by vote, but by the Spirit and by truth.

A sunset for the old barriers.

A sunrise for the people of God—Jew and Gentile, one in Christ.

## "The Yoke Removed"

No iron law, no hardened chain,
No mark of flesh, no ancient claim—
But by the Spirit's wind we rise,
Born of the cross, the Lamb, the skies.

No wall, no court, no distant gate,
No burdened yoke, no fearsome weight—
But open arms and pierced hands,
A kingdom built on freedom's land.

## Reflections from the Road

1. Why was the Council of Jerusalem such a pivotal moment in the history of the church?

2. What dangers would have arisen if Christianity had remained a sect of Judaism?

3. How does understanding this moment deepen our appreciation for salvation by grace through faith alone?

4. In what ways are we still tempted today to "add" conditions to God's grace?

5. How can the Spirit-led decision of the early church guide us in resolving modern tensions with truth and grace?

# 22

# The Bitter Parting

## *Acts 15:36–41*

They stood together after the Council of Jerusalem—brothers in arms, witnesses to the power of grace.

Paul and Barnabas had faced dangers, stones, slander, and shipwrecks of the soul.
They had carried the gospel to places where no one else dared to tread.
They had seen hearts changed, chains broken, churches born.

And now, they planned to go back—to strengthen the believers, to share the Council's verdict, to encourage the growing flock.

But before they could take the first step, they stumbled.

Barnabas wanted to take John Mark—the young cousin he had always believed in, the one who had once deserted them on the first journey.
Paul refused.

The text is stark:
*"They had such a sharp disagreement that they parted company."*
(Acts 15:39)

Paul, ever zealous, ever driven, saw only the risk.
Barnabas, ever patient, ever hopeful, saw the boy behind the mistake.

It was a clash not merely of plans, but of character:

- The builder versus the healer.

- The taskmaster versus the encourager.

- The lion versus the dove.

Who was right?

Perhaps both.
Perhaps neither.
Perhaps that is not even the right question.

The kingdom was not broken by their parting.
In God's strange economy, it was multiplied.

Barnabas took John Mark and sailed for Cyprus, retracing earlier steps.
Paul chose Silas and set out northward, strengthening churches and founding new ones.

Two teams where once there was one.
Two mission fields opened instead of one revisited.

Years later, a graying, battle-worn Paul would write from a Roman prison:

*"Get Mark and bring him with you, because he is helpful to me in my ministry."* (2 Timothy 4:11)

The boy he had once rejected became the man he now longed to see.

> Without Barnabas' second chance, no John Mark.
> Without John Mark's recovery, no Gospel of Mark.
> Without the Gospel of Mark, no shared foundation for Matthew and Luke.

The bitter parting did not have the final word.
Grace did.

## "When Brothers Part"

Two hearts that bled on common road,
Two hands that bore the gospel's load—
Torn not by sword, nor foe, nor fear,
But by the fault lines running near.

One saw the cost, the peril's mark,
One saw the spark within the dark.
One clung to past, one clung to grace—
Both stumbled on the narrow place.

Yet God, who weaves with broken thread,
Still crowned the path they each would tread.


## Reflections from the Road

1. Why do you think God allowed Paul and Barnabas to separate rather than forcing reconciliation at that moment? The question that reverberates: "When brothers disagree... can God still bless the mess?"

2. What does this story teach us about disagreements among faithful believers?

3. How can God's purposes still move forward even when our plans fracture?

4. In your own life, where have you seen grace redeem situations of broken fellowship or painful parting?

5. What qualities of Barnabas' character do you see reflected in John Mark's later restoration and contribution to the church?

# 23

# The Call Forward

## *Acts 15:40–16:10*

The road stretched before them again, dusty and uncertain.

Paul and Silas left Antioch with a mission—to strengthen the young churches and spread the message of grace.
They moved through Syria and Cilicia, hearts burning with purpose.

In Lystra, a new light flickered: Timothy.

Half-Jew, half-Greek, raised in the Scriptures by his mother and grandmother, Timothy was young but faithful.
Paul saw something rare in him—a teachable heart, a steady spirit, a future leader.

Timothy would become more than a companion.
He would become a son—the son Paul never had, a legacy written not in blood, but in faith.

*"You then, my son, be strong in the grace that is in Christ Jesus... And the things you have heard me say in the presence of many witnesses entrust to reliable people who will also be qualified to teach others."* (2 Timothy 2:1–2)

The chain of faith would not end with Paul.
It would stretch forward through Timothy and those he would teach.
The Kingdom multiplies through **discipleship, not celebrity**.

But even as the team grew, clarity shrank.

## Discerning God's Will

Paul, so often decisive, found doors closing.
They were **forbidden by the Spirit** to speak in Asia.
They tried Bithynia—another "no."
They drifted to Troas—no vision, no clear assignment.

For a man like Paul, accustomed to marching orders, the silence must have been unbearable.

It is a hard thing when the called must wait.

But in the waiting, the vision came.

*"During the night Paul had a vision of a man of Macedonia standing and begging him, 'Come over to Macedonia and help us.' After Paul had seen the vision, we got ready at once to leave for Macedonia, concluding that God had called us to preach the gospel to them."* (Acts 16:9–10)

The pronoun shifted: *we*.
Luke had joined them.
The journey moved from guesswork to certainty.


## The Dangerous, Unstoppable Calling

Paul was never more dangerous to the kingdom of darkness than when he knew:

- **He was called and sent,**

- **His message was sure,**

- **His heart burned with love for Jesus and the lost,**

- **And he had the courage to obey.**

Troas marked a turning.
Europe waited.

History pivoted on the obedience of a few weary travelers who refused to quit.

## "When the Way is Closed"

The road was shut, the trail was barred,
The heavens silent, visions marred—
Yet still he walked, though clouded skies,
Still prayed, still hoped, still lifted eyes.

And when the night was deep and long,
A whisper wove itself to song—
"Come help us!" cried the midnight man,
And gospel crossed from sea to land.

## Reflections from the Road

1. How does Paul's relationship with Timothy model the importance of mentoring and spiritual legacy?

2. What can we learn from Paul's patience and persistence when discerning God's direction?

3. Have you ever experienced closed doors leading you to a better, unexpected calling?

4. How does certainty of calling, message, and obedience make a follower of Christ "dangerous" to the powers of darkness?

5. Who in your life might be your "Timothy"—someone you can invest in for the sake of Christ and future generations?

# 24

# The World Turned Upside Down
### *Acts 16:9–40; Acts 17:1–9*

The cry came at night:
*"Come over to Macedonia and help us!"* (Acts 16:9)

Paul answered—and history shifted.

For the first time, the gospel crossed into Europe.
Not by imperial decree.
Not by philosopher's essay.
But by the footsteps of tired missionaries on the shores of Neapolis.

They passed through Philippi, where a businesswoman believed and a demon fled.
They passed through prison bars, where hymns shook stone foundations and hearts alike.
And they came to Thessalonica, where the accusation that would echo across centuries was first hurled:

*"These men who have turned the world upside down have come here too."* (Acts 17:6, NKJV)

They didn't mean it kindly.
But they weren't wrong.

The gospel Paul preached dismantled the world's careful scaffolding:

- Power without justice,

- Religion without truth,

- Empire without mercy.

Paul didn't come to adjust the temperature of society.
He came to shake its very foundation.

The message he carried was not polite reform.
It was revolutionary love—love that crowns Christ King over every counterfeit.

## How the World Was Shaken

If we look closely, the pattern of that upside-down revolution had already begun:

- **Spirit-possessed**: They were led not by master plans, but by divine promptings. (Acts 16:6–8)

- **Vision-driven**: They moved because a midnight cry pierced their hearts. (Acts 16:9)

- **Action-oriented**: They responded immediately, without committee or delay. (Acts 16:10a)

- **Persuaded**: They were confident the mission was God's doing, not their ambition. (Acts 16:10b)

- **Pragmatic**: They chose accessible, cultural entry points for the gospel—sitting by riversides, speaking to women, seeing value where others did not. (Acts 16:12–13)

- **Passionate**: They spoke boldly where the world saw no audience. (Acts 16:13)

- **Powerful**: They confronted darkness directly—and saw it flee. (Acts 16:16–18)

- **Persecuted**: They were beaten, jailed, and accused for disturbing the peace. (Acts 16:19–24)

- **Praising**: They sang hymns in chains. (Acts 16:25)

This was the alchemy of gospel disruption:

**Spirit + Vision + Courage + Praise = Earthquake.**

## Not Rebels—Ambassadors

Paul did not seek to start riots.
He sought to proclaim a Kingdom.

But in a world ruled by idols, injustice, and hollow religion,
**the Kingdom always feels like a revolution.**

And so it was:
Some repented.
Some rioted.
Some ran Paul and Silas out of town.

But the seeds were sown.
And the ground shook under the weight of a new reality breaking in.

The charge still stands today.

## "The Earthquake Within"

Not by sword, nor flag, nor throne,
But Spirit's cry and blood alone—
They turned the world, they shook the skies,
With whispered prayers and martyr's cries.

Not riots raised by rebel bands,
But kingdoms crushed by pierced hands.
And still the tremors roll and rise,
Where love and truth refuse disguise.

### Reflections from the Road

1. What in your life or ministry bears resemblance to this upside-down Kingdom?

2. How do you respond to opposition or accusation? Do you see it as affirmation rather than defeat?

3. What would it look like for your church, family, or small group to be known for "*turning the world upside down*"?

4. In a world hostile to Christ's reign, where is God calling you to sow seeds that might shake the ground beneath your feet?

# 25

# Open Minds and Open Hearts

## *Acts 17:1–15*

The road from Philippi wound south, dusty and worn.
Paul, Silas, and Timothy pressed on, carrying a gospel meant for kings and commoners alike.

In Thessalonica, they found a synagogue—and in it, a spark.

Paul reasoned with the Jews and God-fearers for three Sabbaths, opening the Scriptures, proclaiming:
"*The Christ had to suffer and rise from the dead.*" (Acts 17:3)

Jesus. Crucified. Resurrected. Returning.

It was a message that cut deep.
Some believed—Jews, Greeks, influential women.
But others hardened, stirred a mob, and turned the city into chaos.

Paul was forced to flee.
The fledgling church—barely born—was left with burning questions.

When weeks stretched into months, and Christ did not return,
and some among them **died**, they wrestled with new fears:
"*Have we missed the Kingdom? What happens to those who die before Jesus returns?*"

Those urgent questions would later stir Paul to write **1 and 2 Thessalonians**—some of the earliest Christian writings we possess.
From brevity and heartbreak, God birthed letters of hope and clarity.


From Thessalonica, they slipped away to Berea.
There, the pattern shifted.

The Bereans were **noble**—not because they believed easily,
but because they **searched diligently**.

They questioned.
They investigated.
They opened the Scriptures daily to test what Paul proclaimed.

Their posture was a model for all who seek truth:

- **An open mind to question.**

- **An open Bible to validate**

- **An open heart to believe.**

Many believed—both Jews and Greeks.

But even here, the shadows from Thessalonica followed them.
Agitators stirred unrest, and Paul was forced onward again—this time toward Athens.

The road was hard.
But seeds had been planted.

Some questioned.
Some searched.
Some believed.

The Kingdom grew, even in cracks of opposition and uncertainty.

## "Seeds on Stony Roads"

He sowed on streets where stones were thrown,
On hearts that closed and hearts unknown—
Some questions burned, some praises sang,
Some opened wide, some curses rang.

Yet in the fields of battered ground,
Where mobs rose up and doubts were found,
Still sprouted life the Spirit grew—
Still rain fell down, still morning dew.

## Reflections from the Road

1. How did Paul's brief stay in Thessalonica lead to long-term fruit through his letters?

2. What fears or unanswered questions sometimes shake our faith— and how can we address them through Scripture?

3. What made the Bereans "more noble" than those in Thessalonica?

4. How can we cultivate an open mind, an open Bible, and an open heart in our own search for truth?

5. Where might God be sowing seeds in your life—even along stony or difficult paths?

# 26

# Witness on Mars Hill

## *Acts 17:16–34*

The statues rose around him like silent judges.
Temples towered over every street.
Altars bled smoke into the skies.

Athens, crowned with human achievement, was a city drowning in
idols.

Paul's spirit burned within him.
This was not curiosity.
It was grief.
It was holy agitation.

He followed his pattern:
First, the synagogue—always the covenant people first.
Then, the marketplace—where every voice, every philosophy, every
longing heart collided.

It was there, in the agora, that philosophers overheard him—Stoics,
Epicureans, seekers and skeptics alike.
Intrigued and mocking, they invited him to speak at the Areopa-
gus—Mars Hill, the seat of Athenian thought and judgment.

Here, Paul stood—not in a synagogue, not in a home, but before the
intellectual elites of the ancient world.

**The Message Crafted for the Moment**
Paul did not thunder accusations.

He built a bridge.

- He began with observation: *"I see that you are very religious in all respects."* (Acts 17:22)
- He connected with their own altar: *"To an unknown god."* (Acts 17:23)
- He proclaimed the true God—the Creator, Sustainer, Sovereign.
- He exposed human ignorance—the folly of worshiping the created rather than the Creator.
- He called for repentance—because judgment had been set, and the proof was in the resurrection of Jesus.

Paul modeled what he would later command:
*"Preach the word; be prepared in season and out of season."* (2 Timothy 4:2)
*"Always be ready to give an answer for the hope that is in you."* (1 Peter 3:15)

He stood ready—and he spoke.

### The Response
It was not a mass revival.

- Some sneered at the mention of resurrection.
- Some shrugged it off: *"We will hear you again on this matter."* (Acts 17:32)
- A few believed—among them Dionysius the Areopagite and a woman named Damaris.

This is often the pattern of gospel witness:
- Mockers,
- Fence-sitters,
- True seekers.

Paul did not harvest a great church in Athens.
No epistle bears its name.
No lasting movement is recorded.

But seeds were planted.

The Spirit moves in mysteries, and the harvest often blooms in unexpected soil.

Paul would leave Athens and journey to Corinth—the city of commerce, immorality, and fleshly indulgence.
And there, among the broken, the gospel would find rich, messy ground.

**"The Word in Stone Cities"**
Among the stones and hollow prayers,
He lifted Christ through smoke-filled air—
Not with sword, nor crown, nor rod,
But simple words about his God.

Some laughed. Some leaned. Some turned away.
Some found the light of breaking day.
Not every field yields golden sheaves,
But still the faithful sower leaves.

**Reflections from the Road**
1. How does Paul's approach at Mars Hill model thoughtful, respectful, yet bold gospel witness?
2. Why is it important to be "ready in season and out of season" when opportunities arise?
3. How do you respond when your efforts seem to yield little visible fruit?

4. In your own life, where might God be calling you to sow faithfully—even if the harvest seems distant?

5. What can we learn from the irony that Athens, so full of knowledge, bore little fruit, while Corinth, full of brokenness, would explode with new life?

# 27

# A Season to Build, a Time to Go

## *Acts 18:1–22*

The road from Athens ended at the edge of the sea—Corinth.
A city where flesh reigned and fortunes turned fast.
A city where idols were not carved in stone alone, but walked the streets.

Here, Paul found unlikely allies.

Aquila and Priscilla—refugees from Rome, skilled tentmakers, believers in the gospel.
Whether they had known Christ before or met Him through Paul is unclear.
What is clear is this:
They became friends, partners, and fellow soldiers in the gospel.

Paul worked alongside them with rough hands and stitched cloth,
preaching on Sabbaths, reasoning with the Jews.
The old pattern, familiar and faithful.

But in Corinth, a line was drawn.
After fierce rejection from the synagogue, Paul shook the dust from his garments and declared:

94

*"From now on I will go to the Gentiles!"* (Acts 18:6)

And he did—next door, no less, into the house of Titius Justus.


## A New Phase: The Church Rising from Gentile Soil

Corinth became a turning point.

• Paul stayed for **eighteen months**, longer than almost anywhere else.

• He saw converts, miracles, and slow, stubborn growth.

• Even the synagogue leader, Crispus, believed and was baptized (Acts 18:8).

But friction remained.

The Jews tried to haul Paul before the Roman proconsul Gallio.
They accused him of preaching an illegal religion.

Gallio dismissed the case without even hearing it.
To Paul, it was a decisive, God-sent victory:
The gospel remained free to move.

In the aftermath, the crowd turned on Sosthenes, a synagogue leader—beating him when legal recourse failed.
Later, a man named Sosthenes would greet the Corinthian church alongside Paul (1 Corinthians 1:1).
Was it the same man?
Perhaps.
If so, grace had done its quiet, healing work.


## A Vow, a Vision, and a Farewell

After *"a good while"* longer in Corinth (Acts 18:18), Paul sensed it was time to move.

He had made a vow—likely connected to gratitude for God's protection or a private devotion.
The details are lost to history.
The urgency was not.

Paul, along with Aquila and Priscilla, sailed for Ephesus—the great city of Asia.

In Ephesus, the synagogue doors opened wide.
The Jews urged Paul to stay longer.
Opportunity shone on the horizon.

But the vow bound him.
He promised to return if God permitted (Acts 18:21).

From Ephesus to Caesarea to Jerusalem, Paul closed the Second Missionary Journey with a heart full of unfinished dreams and new visions stirring.

The soil had been tilled.
The road ahead would be even harder—and even richer.

A season to build had ended.
A new time was coming.


### "The Stitching of the Kingdom"

In tents by firelight truths were sewn,
In flesh and cloth and Spirit grown—
The Kingdom spread by calloused hands,
By hearts that heeded still commands.

A season built, a door swung wide,
A vow pressed hard, the ships would glide—
But echoes of the gospel sown
Would stretch beyond what eyes had known.

## Reflections from the Road

1. How does Paul's time in Corinth show that the gospel can flourish even in the most broken places?

2. What does the emergence of Aquila and Priscilla teach us about the value of partnerships in ministry?

3. Why was Paul's decision to focus more intentionally on Gentiles such a significant turning point?

4. How do vows, promises, or personal devotions still shape the way God leads us today?

5. What opportunities might be "waiting in Ephesus" in your own life—future fields that God is preparing while you are faithful in your present work?

## Transition

At this point in the journey, our treatment of the storyline of Acts pauses—but Paul's voice carries on.

From Corinth, with his heart still tethered to the young believers in Thessalonica, he wrote two of his earliest letters. What he could not finish face to face, he finished in ink—strengthening their faith, answering their questions, and calling them to live with courage between the now and the not yet.

# 28

# A Young Church in Waiting

The city of Thessalonica hummed with energy, commerce, and devotion to the old gods. It was a place where Roman power, Greek philosophy, and diverse religions mingled in the streets. Into this vibrant but restless world, Paul stepped — carrying a message unlike any the synagogue or marketplace had ever heard: the Messiah had come, had risen, and would return.

Paul's time in Thessalonica was heartbreakingly brief. For three Sabbaths — perhaps no more than two or three weeks — he reasoned with the Jews and preached to the Gentiles. A small but passionate church sprang to life, composed of Jews, God-fearing Greeks, and leading women of the city. But jealousy flared. Opposition grew fierce. Paul was forced to leave, his heart still bound to the newborn church he had scarcely begun to nourish.

From Corinth, Paul's concern for the Thessalonians burned within him. Had their faith survived the storm? Were they still clinging to Christ? Timothy was dispatched to find out — and his return brought a mixture of joy and alarm. The Thessalonians had endured, yes. But questions, grief, and confusion gnawed at them. Some among them had died. What would happen to these beloved brothers and sisters? Had they missed the Lord's return? And among the living, some had begun to idle — withdrawing from work, waiting passively for the skies to open.

Paul's first letter answered with urgency and tenderness. He praised their endurance, comforted their fears about death, and called them to live honorably as they awaited Christ's coming. His words in *1 Thessalonians 5:14* gave a compact charge: *"Admonish the idle, en-*

*courage the fainthearted, help the weak, be patient with them all."* It was a blueprint for the messy, beautiful work of a church living between two worlds — the present age and the age to come.

Yet confusion lingered. False teachers soon exploited their hopes and fears, claiming the Day of the Lord had already dawned. Anxiety deepened, and disorder grew. Paul, still burning with pastoral love, wrote again. In *2 Thessalonians*, he corrected falsehoods, reassured the faithful, and exhorted them to stand firm and work diligently while waiting for the true, glorious unveiling of Christ.

Together, these two letters form a portrait of a young church under pressure — a people learning, as all believers must, how to hope, how to wait, and how to live faithfully when the timetable of heaven seems hidden. Paul, their spiritual father, pointed them — and us — not only to an event on the horizon, but to a life of active readiness, love, and perseverance today.

### "Between Two Worlds"

They heard Your voice in the marketplace,
They wept when the news was true;
They stood in the dust of a broken world,
And learned how to wait for You.

Their hearts were lit with living flame,
Their hands were scarred with stone,
They watched the sky, they mended nets,
They learned to trust alone.

Between what was and what will be,
They lived with lifted eyes—
Teaching us still to hope, to work,
And watch the eastern skies.

1. How does Paul's deep concern for the Thessalonians encourage you about the nature of spiritual leadership today?

2. In what ways do you see the tension between "waiting" and "working" in your own spiritual life?

3. What fears or confusions about the future most challenge your faith right now? How does Paul's message to Thessalonica speak into those fears?

4. First Thessalonians 5:14 gives four pastoral instructions. Which of these is most needed in your life—or through your life into others—right now?

5. What might it look like for you to "live between two worlds" with faithfulness, purpose, and joy?

# 29

# Hope for Those Who Sleep

## *1 Thessalonians 4:13–18*

Grief clung to the young believers of Thessalonica like a low mist. They had embraced the gospel with joy — a living hope in a risen Christ who had promised to return. But now some of their number had died. Friends. Family. Believers who had been waiting, watching. Had they missed the promise? Would death separate them forever from the kingdom they longed to see?

Paul wrote not to diminish their sorrow, but to reshape it. Grief was not forbidden; it was transformed. "*We do not want you to be unin-*

*formed*" he said, "*so that you will not grieve as indeed the rest of mankind do, who have no hope.*" Death was not the end of the road. Those who "slept" in Christ would rise at His coming — first to greet Him, first to share in His triumph.

With vivid language, Paul lifted their eyes: the Lord descending from heaven, the shout of command, the trumpet of God, the dead in Christ rising, the living caught up to meet Him in the air. It was not a secret or private event; it was a cosmic victory parade. The King was coming. The family of God would be gathered — not in death, but in life everlasting.

Paul's final word on the matter was pastoral, not theoretical: "*Therefore encourage one another with these words.*" Theology was never an end in itself for Paul. It was always fuel for faith, courage for the heart, strength for the weary.
Grief, yes — but grief shot through with glory.
Tears, yes — but tears that would be wiped away in a world remade by love.


Yet even beyond the comfort Paul offered the grieving brothers and sisters in Thessalonica, there is a deeper mystery revealed by Christ. Eternal life is not merely a future promise; it is a present possession. "*Whoever believes in Me has everlasting life,*" Jesus said — not someday, but now.

From our human perspective, events like the return of Christ and the resurrection are still future. We live in hope, trusting that our future with God is sure and certain. That hope lightens our burden even in sorrow, as Paul assured the Thessalonians.

But from God's perspective, everything is present. That is why God told Moses to say, "*I AM*" — the ever-present One — had sent him. God transcends time and space. Those who believe in Him have life in its fullness, beginning now. We do not wait to receive eternal life;

it is ours the moment we are birthed from above.

In his second letter to the Corinthians, Paul would open this mystery more fully. He wrote, *"To be absent from the body is to be present with the Lord,"* and spoke of death not as being unclothed, but clothed anew in a *"house not made with hands."*

In the realm of God, where time bends and eternity embraces the soul, death is not a waiting room. It is a doorway — a transition from shadow to substance, from faith to sight, from life begun to life fulfilled.

A friend stated the truth of Christian death in this way:

*"At death, the believer steps out of time and into eternity, experiencing the fullness of God's promise without delay — even though from earth's perspective, the story still unfolds in measured steps."*


## "Not the End"

The grave is not a prison,
The night is not the end;
The sleeper wakes to morning's light,
At the summons of a Friend.

The trumpet sounds, the skies are torn,
The shadows flee away;
And those who sleep in Christ shall rise
Into eternal day.


## Reflections from the Road

1. How does Christian hope transform the way we experience grief and loss?

2. What images in Paul's description (1 Thess. 4:13–18) most stir your imagination and strengthen your faith?

3. In what ways can you encourage others with the promise of Christ's return today?

4. How might this vision of resurrection change your priorities or perspective on daily life?

5, What habits or practices help you live with an eye toward the coming Kingdom rather than being trapped by the present moment?

# 30

# Living in the Light

## *1 Thessalonians 5:1–11*

The Thessalonian believers lived in a world dark with uncertainty. Empires rose and fell. Rumors of war, famine, betrayal, and suffering filled the air. It would have been easy — and understandable — for them to withdraw, to live anxiously on the margins of life, waiting for the promised return of Christ.

But Paul painted a different vision.
They were not called to cower in the shadows, nor to idle in anxious expectation.
They were **children of the day**, bearers of a light that would not be extinguished even by death or disaster.

*"The Day of the Lord will come like a thief in the night,"* he warned — sudden, unexpected to those who live asleep in darkness. But not to the children of light. They were to be alert, sober, armed with the breastplate of faith and love, and the helmet of the hope of salvation.

Waiting, for Paul, was not passive. It was vigilant. It was not hiding;

it was living — courageously, joyfully, expectantly.

The church was not meant to be a bunker for the fearful but a lighthouse for the world.

They were to be awake, active, and luminous — signs of the Kingdom breaking into a weary world.

And so are we.

## "Awake in the Dawn"

Not in the hush of trembling fear,
Nor in the dark of flight,
We stand with open, lifted hearts—
Children born of light.

The trumpet sounds, the shadows break,
The morning cracks the skies;
And every heart that dared to hope
Will rise, and rise, and rise.

This call to live alert and ready echoes the parables Jesus once told. The wise virgins kept their lamps burning, the faithful servants labored with the master's gifts, the true sheep loved without even knowing they served the King. Paul was not inventing a new way of waiting; he was passing on the life Christ had already described — a life awake, working, loving, shining until the day dawned in full.

The Thessalonians were to be awake, active, and luminous — signs of the Kingdom already pressing into the world.

And so are we.

## Reflections from the Road

1. What does it mean to live as a "child of the day" in a world often shrouded in darkness?

2. How is Paul's picture of waiting for Christ's return different from passively withdrawing from the world?

3. What habits or practices help you stay alert, sober, and anchored in faith, love, and hope?

4. In what ways can your life be a "lighthouse" to others right now?

5. How does the hope of Christ's return shape your daily courage and endurance?

# 31

# Stand Firm in Troubled Times

## *2 Thessalonians 2:1–17*

**Focal Passage:** "*So then, brothers and sisters, stand firm and hold on to the traditions which you were taught, whether by word of mouth or by letter from us.*" (2 Thessalonians 2:15)

**Core Situation:**

• After Paul's first letter, confusion still lingered about the Day of the Lord.

• False teachings spread — including claims that the Day had already come.

• Anxiety and disorder deepened.

• Paul corrects their understanding, reassures them, and exhorts them to **stand firm** — not shifting with every rumor or fear.

Fear spreads faster than truth.

Not long after Paul's first letter, a fresh wave of anxiety swept through the church in Thessalonica. Whispers and forged letters claimed the Day of the Lord had already come. Confused, shaken, and still learning how to walk by faith, the Thessalonian believers struggled to understand. Had they been left behind? Had the promises failed? Was everything they had hoped for slipping away?

Paul answered with clarity and pastoral urgency.
The Day of the Lord had not come. Certain events — rebellion, the rise of the lawless one — must happen first. But more importantly, the Thessalonians were called not to live by rumor, but by rooted faith.

"*Stand firm,*" Paul urged them.
Hold fast to what you have been taught — not just by words whispered in fear, but by the living truth you received from our own lips and letters.
Paul did not invite speculation about hidden mysteries. He called them to stand on revealed truth. The anchor for troubled times was not speculation about the future but steadfastness in the gospel already given.

Paul reminded them that they had been **chosen**, **loved**, and **called** — not to fear, but to glory.
And in that assurance, they could endure anything — storms of persecution, waves of confusion, even the slow grind of waiting.

The true children of the day do not chase shadows.
They stand, they shine, they hold fast — until the real dawn breaks.

## "Hold Fast"

When fear sweeps down like sudden storm,
And voices darkly swarm,
Hold fast to light, hold fast to love,
Hold fast through every harm.

The promises are not undone,
The morning will not fail;
The King who calls us to endure
Will bid us lift the veil.

## Reflections from the Road

1. What made the Thessalonian believers vulnerable to fear and confusion? What makes us vulnerable today?

2. What does it mean to "*stand firm*" when the culture around us is anxious, hostile, or misleading?

3. How can you strengthen your hold on the truth of the gospel in everyday life?

4. Why is it important to remember that we are "*loved by the Lord*" and "*called to share in His glory*" (2 Thess. 2:13–14)?

5. What are some ways you can be a steady, faithful presence for others during times of uncertainty?

# 32

## A Worker Well Prepared

### *Acts 18:23–28*

The Third Missionary Journey began not with fanfare,
but with footsteps—Paul retracing the dusty trails of his earlier
work, strengthening the fledgling churches scattered across Galatia
and Phrygia.

It was the shepherd's heart in him.
The builder returning to fortify the walls he had raised.

But while Paul pressed westward, another figure was rising further
to the west in Ephesus, the great city of Asia minor. Apollos.

A Jew from Alexandria—one of the greatest learning centers of the
ancient world—Apollos arrived in Ephesus, bearing a rare combination of gifts:

- **Eloquent** in speech, able to capture hearts and minds.

- **Mighty** in the Scriptures, not merely knowing the text, but
wielding it with strength.

- **Fervent** in spirit, burning with zeal for God.

- **Diligent** in his teaching, passionate for truth.

- **Courageous** in public proclamation, unashamed of the gospel.

- **Teachable**, willing to receive correction and grow deeper.

- **Fruitful**, building up the body wherever he served.

But his knowledge, though sincere, was incomplete. He knew only
the baptism of John—a gospel of repentance, but not yet the fullness
of Christ crucified and risen.

## The Gift of Discipleship

It was here that Aquila and Priscilla stepped forward.
Together—husband and wife, co-laborers in Christ—they took
Apollos aside.

They did not humiliate him.
They did not silence him.

They *"explained to him the way of God more perfectly."* (Acts
18:26)

They filled in the missing pieces with grace and truth.
They discipled a diamond in the rough into a powerful tool for the
Kingdom.

In an age when women's voices were often silenced by culture,
Priscilla's inclusion as a teacher stands quietly, firmly, beautifully.

In God's vineyard, gifts are not buried by gender, but cultivated for
His glory.


## A Brother Commended

Equipped and eager, Apollos determined to cross the sea to Achaia.
The believers in Ephesus did something precious:
They wrote letters of recommendation on his behalf.

In the early church, faithfulness traveled with testimony.
No one served alone or untested.
The body recognized and affirmed its workers.

And Apollos proved worthy of their trust.

He greatly helped those who had believed through grace.
He powerfully refuted the Jews in public debate, demonstrating from
the Scriptures that Jesus was the Christ.

A planter had gone forth before him. Apollos watered. And God
gave the increase.

## "The Fire and the Fervor"

A voice rose strong where echoes slept,
A heart aflame, a word well kept—
Yet tender hands in shadow's light
Revealed the fullness of the fight.

No shame, no pride, no boast, no chain,
Just Spirit's fire and truth's refrain—
A worker shaped for fields untold,
A fervent flame, a heart made bold.


## Reflections from the Road

1. How does Apollos' teachability model a critical virtue for Christian growth?

2. What can we learn from Aquila and Priscilla's approach to mentoring a rising leader?

3. Why is it important for churches to affirm and commend faithful workers?

4. In what ways might God be calling you to *"explain the way more perfectly"* to someone around you?

5. How do Apollos' traits—eloquence, Scripture knowledge, fervor, humility—challenge and inspire your own walk of faith?

# 33

# The Gates of Ephesus

## *Acts 18:23–19:7*

Paul had traveled this road before.

After sharing his reports with the faithful congregation at Antioch—
just as he had done at the end of his first missionary journey—Paul
traveled a familiar road strengthening the young churches across
Galatia and Phrygia.
Once he had accomplished that, he set his face toward Ephesus.

He had seen the opportunity on his brief visit before.
Now he came determined to seize it.

## Ephesus: A City Like No Other

Ephesus was no small outpost.
It was a roaring crossroads of empire—a city of commerce, culture,
and religion unmatched in Asia Minor.

Four great roads funneled goods from across the land.
Ships unloaded treasures from distant shores.

The markets overflowed with every imaginable luxury—and with
human lives.
Ephesus was the capital of the ancient slave trade.

Above all, it was a religious city—dominated by the towering Temple of Artemis, one of the Seven Wonders of the Ancient World.

Pilgrims streamed into the city to seek favor from the goddess.

A guild of silversmiths grew rich crafting miniature shrines for the
faithful.

Wealth, superstition, spectacle—the soul of Ephesus was captive to idols.

Into this stronghold, Paul came bearing only the Word of Christ.

## An Unusual Beginning

At the edge of the city, Paul encountered a small group of disciples—followers of John the Baptist's teaching.

They knew repentance.
They knew expectancy.

But they did not yet know the fullness of Christ's finished work.

*"Did you receive the Holy Spirit when you believed?"* Paul asked. (Acts 19:2)

Their blank faces gave the answer.

They had not even heard of the Holy Spirit.

Paul explained the fullness of the gospel—of Jesus crucified, risen, ascended, and sending His Spirit.

They were baptized into the name of Jesus.
Paul laid hands upon them.
And the Spirit came with visible signs—tongues and prophecy, as on Pentecost and Samaria before.

## A Word About the Signs

These moments of outward manifestation were **not normative** for every believer.
They were **signposts**—markers from God at pivotal transitions:

- Pentecost in Jerusalem (Acts 2),

- The breakthrough among the Samaritans (Acts 8),

- The gospel going to Gentiles (Acts 10),

- The opening of Ephesus to the full gospel (Acts 19).

At each point, God confirmed that the gospel was advancing into new territory.

The Spirit's power is always at work,
but His manifestations vary according to God's purposes—not human command.

True Christianity is measured not by ecstatic signs, but by transformed lives.


**The City Awaits**
Twelve men stood with Paul that day.
Twelve—like the apostles, like the tribes of Israel.

A new work was about to unfold.
Not by force.
Not by spectacle.

But by truth.
By Spirit.
By the Word of Christ.

The gates of Ephesus had opened.

The battle for a continent had begun.


**"The Threshold of Thunder"**
Where idols towered, hearts were chained,
Where gold and gods and greed remained—
A voice like river's roar did fall,
"Christ alone is Lord of all!"

Twelve stood firm on battered stone,
A spark, a seed, a cornerstone—

And gates that boasted iron and pride,
Would tremble where the Spirit cried.


## Reflections from the Road

1. Why was Ephesus such a strategic city for Paul's mission?

2. How does Paul's encounter with the disciples of John show the importance of both truth and pastoral care?

3. Why were extraordinary manifestations (tongues, prophecy) given at certain moments in the early church—and why are they not the standard measure of faith today?

4. In what ways does entering a new phase of life or ministry feel like standing at the gates of Ephesus—stepping into challenge and opportunity?

5. How can you prepare yourself, like Paul, to carry the gospel boldly into spiritually resistant places?

# Interlude: When a City Turns

## *A Pause Before Ephesus and Beyond*

Ephesus was more than a city.
For Paul, it became a center of gravity.

Here the apostle found not only a platform but a proving ground. For two full years, he taught daily in the Hall of Tyrannus—sowing gospel truth into a culture saturated with magic, wealth, power, and fear. It wasn't spectacle that changed the city. It was **steady, Spirit-led faithfulness**.

The result?
A spiritual fault line formed under the surface of everyday life.

Scrolls of sorcery were burned in public repentance.
Exorcists failed to mimic Paul's authority and fled in shame.
Merchants of idolatry panicked as their profits waned.
And behind it all, the Word of the Lord *grew mightily and prevailed* (Acts 19:20).

Ephesus became a radiating center.
What Paul taught here would ripple outward—reaching the seven churches later addressed by John in Revelation… preparing the way for the gospel to spread through all Asia… and pushing Paul's heart toward new frontiers.

As the movement grew, so did the resistance.
A riot shook the amphitheater. For two hours, the crowd chanted, *"Great is Artemis of the Ephesians!"*
The gospel had not merely converted individuals.
It had *confronted the city's gods*.

Yet in all this, Paul was not chasing drama. He was dreaming beyond it.

As the season in Ephesus closed, his eyes turned west—toward **Jerusalem**, **Rome**, and even **Spain**. The gospel was gaining ground. And Paul was preparing to hand the mission off to others, trusting the seeds sown in tears would reap joy far beyond his reach.

### Persistence

Paul stayed longer in Ephesus than in almost any other city. He taught, discipled, reasoned, and confronted error—not with flair, but with enduring clarity. The gospel grew, not because of signs alone, but through sustained proclamation.

### Power

The gospel didn't just challenge personal sin; it **toppled spiritual strongholds**. Magic was renounced. Darkness was exposed. The name of Jesus was lifted high, and the counterfeit powers of the age were left trembling.

### Pressure

The riot in Ephesus was not a setback—it was a symptom. When the gospel challenges cultural idols, resistance is inevitable. What threatened Demetrius wasn't Paul's preaching alone—it was the economic collapse of Artemis worship. When the gospel moves, **idols feel the heat**.

### Progression

Even as God worked mightily in Ephesus, Paul was already preparing for what came next. He sent Timothy and Erastus ahead into Macedonia. He spoke of Jerusalem. He dreamed of Rome. And in the winter to come, he would write the letter to the Romans—his theological masterpiece and missionary manifesto.

The third missionary journey was more than a loop on a map. **It was a deepening of the mission.**

A broadening of the vision.
A prelude to legacy.

## "The Sound of Burning Pages"

They gathered scrolls by lamplight's glow,
Where charms and chains had bound the soul—
And in the square they lit a flame,
To cleanse the past, to change the name.
A blaze was born no hand could tame,
A Kingdom spread, a world aflame.

## Reflections from the Road

1, Why do you think Paul stayed in Ephesus so long compared to other cities? What does this teach us about patient ministry?

2. What idols—economic, cultural, personal—still tremble when the gospel truly moves in a community?

3. Have you ever witnessed the gospel shake a system, not just a person? What happened?

4. In what ways did Paul prepare others to continue the mission beyond him? Who are you preparing

5. What "next horizon" might the Spirit be stirring in you, even while you're still standing faithfully where you are?

# 34

# When the Darkness Breaks

## *Acts 19:11–20*

*"I do not run like a man running aimlessly; I do not fight like a man beating the air."* (1 Corinthians 9:26)

Paul was no shadow boxer.
And in Acts 19:11–20, we see one of the clearest moments where **the real battle**—against darkness, idolatry, and deception—comes fully into view.

Paul's daily teaching in the Hall of Tyrannus was no dry lecture.
It was the forging of spiritual weapons.

For two years he sowed, and now the harvest began to quake the city.

God was doing *extraordinary* miracles through Paul:

• Handkerchiefs and aprons touched his skin and carried healing to the sick.

• Evil spirits fled at the presence of Christ's authority.

But not all who witnessed these things understood.

Some, like the sons of Sceva—itinerant Jewish exorcists—tried to wield the name of Jesus like a magic incantation.

*"I adjure you by Jesus whom Paul proclaims,"* they cried.

The demon laughed—*"Jesus I know, and Paul I recognize—but who are you?"* (Acts 19:15)

The possessed man leapt upon them with terrifying force.
They fled, naked and bleeding.

The incident spread like fire through Ephesus.
Fear fell on all, and the name of the Lord Jesus was magnified.

## When True Repentance Costs Something

Many who had believed now came forward,
confessing their former practices.

Sorcerers, magicians, and idolaters—
they brought their scrolls,
their costly instruments of deception,
and **burned them publicly**.

The value of the materials destroyed would have equaled 50,000
silver coins—a fortune.

But to them, Christ was worth more.

They did not add Jesus to their old lives.
They laid the old lives down in ashes at His feet.

*"Thus the word of the Lord grew mightily and prevailed."* (Acts
19:20)

The darkness did not collapse all at once.
It cracked, splintered, and finally gave way under the persistent, patient, powerful advance of the gospel.

## The Power Behind the Breakthrough

Notice what broke the stronghold of Ephesus:

- Not political power.

- Not economic leverage.

- Not angry mobs or human schemes.

It was **persistent gospel teaching**,
**authentic spiritual authority**,
and **costly, visible repentance** among the believers themselves.

This is always the pattern of true spiritual revolution:

- Teach the Word daily.

- Live the Word visibly.

- Let the Word cut down the idols.

And when it does, even the strongest fortresses fall.

### "Ashes on the Streets"

The scrolls that whispered secret lies
Were cast upon the flame.
The hands once bound by shadowed ties
Now bore another Name.

The smoke rose up like broken chains,
The embers laughed and cried—
For darkness trembles not at swords,
But where the Truth abides.

### Reflections from the Road

1. Why do you think God sometimes allows extraordinary miracles to accompany the spread of the gospel in new territories?

2. What warning can we draw from the failed exorcism by the sons of Sceva?

3. How does true repentance today still require public, costly renunciations of old ways?

4. What strongholds in our culture—and in our lives—can only be broken by persistent gospel truth and Spirit-empowered living?

5. How does Paul's quiet, daily teaching ministry become the launchpad for massive spiritual breakthroughs?

## Acts pauses; Paul's letters speak

While Paul ministered in Ephesus, a contingency from the Corinthian church came. They reported problems in the congregation. Paul took time to address these problems of division and abuses in worship and some questions that the church had about marriage relationships, eating meat that had been offered to idols, and theological questions like the resurrection. It is time to pause the Acts narrative and hear Paul's voice as it poured out to one of his most complicated and beloved congregations: the church in Corinth.

# 35

# Letters to a Church on the Edge

## *Overview of 1 & 2 Corinthians*

If the early church had a problem child, it was Corinth.

This city was bursting with life—trade, art, ambition, sensuality. It was a place of rising voices, rising tensions, and rising pride. The church that took root there had spiritual gifts in abundance, but spiritual maturity in short supply. They had the Spirit, but not yet the mind of Christ.

Paul loved them fiercely—and wrote to them with fire.

The first letter came after he received reports from Chloe's household and a written plea from the congregation itself. The church was fracturing into factions, tolerating sin, mishandling worship, and misusing spiritual gifts. Paul's tone was urgent, surgical, and sometimes stern—but always pastoral. He was calling them not just to behave better, but to **become who they already were in Christ**.

The second letter followed a different kind of crisis. Paul had sent Timothy to help, and the response was mixed. Some repented. Others questioned Paul's authority altogether. Second Corinthians is Paul at his most vulnerable—and most forceful. He bares his soul, recounts his suffering, and reasserts his apostleship not with bravado, but with scars.

*"We have this treasure in jars of clay,"* he writes. *"When I am weak, then I am strong."*

Together, these two letters offer a gritty, glorious view of church life in the real world.

They speak to **conflict**, **giftedness**, **love**, **suffering**, **leadership**, and **resurrection hope**.

They reveal a church stumbling toward holiness—and an apostle pouring himself out to keep them anchored in the gospel.

## "Letters to the Fractured"

He wrote to those who knew the cross,
Yet still could not forgive—
Who sang in tongues, but crushed with pride,
And fought to seem alive.

He called them not to rise by strength,
But bend beneath the flame—
To walk the way of love again,
And lift the Savior's name.

## Reflections from the Road

1. Why do you think Paul was so emotionally invested in the Corinthians—what does that say about his heart for the church?

2. Have you ever experienced a church that was both vibrant and broken? How does Corinth help us view that tension?

3. What lessons can we draw from how Paul balances correction with compassion?

4. Why is it important to see both of these letters together rather than in isolation?

5. What does Corinth teach us about the challenge of living faithfully in a city—or a culture—filled with power, pride, and distraction?

# 36

# The Foolishness of the Cross

## *1 Corinthians 1:18–25*

The Corinthians loved wisdom.
They came from a city where orators packed the forums and philosophers dined on applause. Sharp minds and sharper tongues ruled the day. To them, truth had to sound impressive—smooth, complex, cultured. They were drawn to charisma, intellect, and status.

Then Paul came preaching a crucified man.

To the world, the cross was an emblem of defeat—shameful, humiliating, weak. A naked man nailed to wood? That was the death of criminals, not kings. The message Paul brought didn't win debates; it made people scoff.

"*Foolishness,*" they said. "*Madness.*"

But Paul refused to dress it up.

He didn't try to make the gospel palatable to Greco-Roman tastes. He proclaimed the cross because it *was* the power of God—the strange, upside-down power that breaks pride, shatters illusions, and saves the soul.

To the Jews, a crucified Messiah was a stumbling block.
To the Greeks, it was foolishness.
But to those being saved, it was the very wisdom and power of God.

The message hasn't changed.

We still live in a world impressed by the loud, the strong, the successful. But the gospel speaks through weakness, humility, sacrifice, and love.

It confounds the wise. It raises the dead.

It begins at the foot of a cross—and leads to the resurrection of the world.

## "Not As We Would Choose"

Not on a throne of polished gold,
But splintered wood and sky grown cold—
He reigned, and bled, and bore the shame,
And triumphed by a cursed name.

No crown of laurel on His brow,
But thorns, and silence, mocked somehow—
Yet this is where the strong are slain,
And fools become the wise again.

## Reflections from the Road

1. Why do you think Paul chose not to "dress up" the gospel for his audience in Corinth?

2. does the cross challenge today's ideas of power, success, or influence?

3. Have you ever been tempted to make your faith more "acceptable" to others? How does this passage reframe that?

4. What does it mean to see the cross as both foolishness to the world and power to the believer?

5. In what ways can the cross shape not just your beliefs, but your way of life?

# 37

# When Love Restrains

## *1 Corinthians 8–10, with 13 as the ethical compass*

Corinth was a place of knowledge, liberty, and pride. In that atmosphere, the Christians who had come to understand their freedom in Christ were flaunting it—especially regarding food sacrificed to idols. To them, idols were nothing. Meat was meat. Why should they restrict themselves for the sake of others who were "weaker" in conscience? And especially when you could get a good steak for cheap.

Paul agreed that idols were nothing. He agreed that, technically, they had a right to eat. But then he said something shocking:

*"If food causes my brother to stumble, I will never eat meat again."* (1 Cor. 8:13)

This wasn't cowardice. It was **love**.

Paul didn't argue for tighter rules. He argued for a **wider heart**.

Christian freedom, rightly understood, is not about doing whatever we want. It is about being so secure in Christ that we can lay down our rights for the sake of others. Not from fear, but from love. Not from law, but from grace.

In chapter 9, Paul uses himself as the example. He had every right to receive support, to take a wife, to be honored. Yet he gave it all up for the sake of the gospel. In chapter 10, he draws the warning line: Don't let liberty become license. What may be lawful is not always beneficial.

And through it all, the ethic that undergirds Paul's teaching is what he declares so powerfully in chapter 13:

*Love is patient. Love is kind. Love does not boast. Love does not seek its own.*

In Corinth, love was not missing because people were weak. It was missing because people were strong—and refused to restrain themselves for the sake of others. Paul showed them a better way: the way of **voluntary self-limitation**, the way of *agape*.

This kind of love is not about emotion. It's about **maturity**. It's the spiritual gift that governs all other gifts. It is the sign not of what we know, but of who we are becoming in Christ.

### "The Strong Who Choose the Low"

I could eat, and still be clean—
Bow to none and speak unseen.
I could boast of what I know,
And trample those who grow too slow.

But love steps back, and love stands still—
To spare the heart, to guard the will.
The cross was not a right reclaimed,
But strength poured out, and self unnamed.

### Reflections from the Road

1. What does Paul mean when he says, "*Knowledge puffs up, but love builds up*" (1 Cor. 8:1)?

2. Have you ever insisted on your freedom or rights, only to realize it hurt someone else spiritually?

3. How does Paul model restraint in chapter 9? What does that say about leadership?

4. How can the ethic of 1 Corinthians 13 guide decisions in areas where believers disagree?

5. What might it look like today to voluntarily limit your freedom for the sake of love?

# 38

# Grace Gifts and Worship Gone Awry

## *1 Corinthians 12–14*

The church in Corinth had charisma, but it lacked character.

In their worship gatherings, spiritual gifts flowed freely—tongues, prophecy, ecstatic speech, demonstrations of power. But Paul saw disorder, pride, and spiritual one-upmanship. The gifts meant to build up the body had become tools for self-promotion. Worship, instead of uniting the church, was dividing it.

That is why Paul devoted three full chapters to course-correcting their understanding. He did not discourage the use of spiritual gifts; rather, he grounded them in their proper source and purpose. Gifts were not badges of spiritual superiority. They were grace-gifts, given by the Spirit, distributed as He wills, for the benefit of all.

**Chapter 12** lays the theological foundation: many gifts, one Spirit; many members, one body. Every believer has a role, and no gift is greater than another.

Chapter 13 shifts the focus to love—not romantic love or sentimental feeling, but agape: the self-giving love that mirrors Christ. Without love, Paul says, all the gifts amount to nothing. Prophecies will cease, tongues will fall silent, knowledge will fade. Love alone will endure.

Chapter 14 turns to practical guidance: worship must be orderly, intelligible, and edifying. Paul urges clarity over confusion, meaning over mystery. Tongues must be interpreted. Prophets must speak in turn. Women, who may have been sources of some of the chaos, were asked to refrain from disruptive speech. The Spirit may inspire, but He does not incite chaos.

The Corinthian church needed this wisdom, and so do we. Spiritual gifts are not about spotlighting ourselves. They are about building up the body and pointing people to Christ. Love is the frame through which every gift must pass. Worship must reflect not just freedom, but maturity.

**"Charisma and the Cross"**

Gifts that dazzle, tongues that sing,
Miracles on rushing wing—
All fall silent, all grow dim,
If love does not reside within.

The hand, the foot, the voice, the eye,
Each with grace the Lord supplies.
But none can boast, and none can reign,
When love is lost, and pride remains.

So worship not in noise alone—
Let order, peace, and truth be shown.
The Spirit speaks through gifts we share,
But only love will keep them fair.

### Reflections from the Road

1. What is the purpose of spiritual gifts according to 1 Corinthians 12–14?

2. Why do you think Paul inserted a chapter on love (chapter 13) in the middle of his teaching on gifts?

3. How does Paul balance freedom in the Spirit with order in the church?

4. In what ways can spiritual gifts be misused in today's church? What safeguards does Paul recommend?

5. How can love serve as both the motivation and the measure of our ministry?

# 39

# Christ the Firstfruits

## *1 Corinthians 15:1–26, 50–58*

For all the passion and controversy swirling through the Corinthian church, Paul saved his longest and most majestic argument for the end: **the resurrection**.

Some believers in Corinth had begun to waver. Maybe the resurrection wasn't literal. Maybe it was only spiritual, metaphorical—a symbol of new life or moral renewal. The idea of actual bodies rising from the grave seemed foolish to some, especially in a Greco-Roman culture that saw the body as inferior, something to escape.

Paul would have none of it.

The resurrection, he insists, is **the very core of the gospel**. Without it, our preaching is useless, our faith is empty, and we are still in our sins. If Christ has not been raised, then death has the last word, and we are to be pitied more than anyone.

But Christ *has* been raised. And in that single historical moment, a new creation began. He is the "*firstfruits*" of those who have fallen asleep—the guarantee that the harvest is coming. As in Adam all die, so in Christ all will be made alive.

This wasn't abstract theology for Paul. This was hope anchored in reality.

He moves from proclamation to promise: what is sown in weakness will be raised in power. The perishable will put on the imperishable. Mortality will be swallowed up by victory. The trumpet will sound, the dead will rise, and we will be changed.

And so, Paul concludes with one of the most triumphant refrains in all of Scripture:

"*Death has been swallowed up in victory.*"

"*O death, where is your victory? O death, where is your sting?*"

"*The sting of death is sin, and the power of sin is the law. But thanks be to God, who gives us the victory through our Lord Jesus Christ.*"

And then, with pastoral tenderness and apostolic force, he closes:

"*Therefore, my beloved brothers and sisters, be steadfast, immovable, always abounding in the work of the Lord, knowing that your labor in the Lord is not in vain.*"

Resurrection is not just about the end. It is fuel for faithfulness now.

### "First Light"

The stone rolled back, the veil undone,
The tomb where death had made its claim—
Now burst with light, for death has failed,
And life has risen in His name.

The seed once sown in broken ground
Now stands in glory, crowned and bright.
And we who mourn shall rise like Him,
Transformed by grace, clothed in His light.


### Reflections from the Road

1. Why was it so essential for Paul to defend the bodily resurrection in Corinth?

2. How does calling Jesus the "firstfruits" shape our view of life after death?

3. What parts of 1 Corinthians 15 bring you the most hope, or stir your faith?

4. How does resurrection power impact the way we live now, not just how we hope to die?

5. What does it mean to be "steadfast and immovable" in the work of the Lord in light of resurrection hope?


### Note on Timing and Location

About a year passed between Paul's first and second letters to the Corinthians.

The first was written from Ephesus, during his extended ministry there.

The second came from Macedonia, as Paul journeyed north to visit the churches there.

It was during this time that he met Titus—fresh from Corinth—with news that would both relieve and rekindle Paul's deep concern for the church he loved. Upon receiving the news from Titus, his assistant, Paul penned 2 Corinthians.

# 40

# Living Letters

## *2 Corinthians 2:14–3:18*

Paul had known defeat, slander, imprisonment, and personal heartbreak. And yet, in a moment of stunning confidence, he bursts into praise:

*"Thanks be to God, who always leads us in triumph in Christ."* (2 Cor. 2:14)

This isn't cheap triumphalism. It is **unquenchable optimism** rooted in a gospel that overcomes everything.

Paul saw himself and his companions as incense bearers in a Roman triumphal procession—the gospel diffusing the aroma of Christ wherever they went. For some, the fragrance brought life. For others, it exposed death. But always, it was powerful. Always, it had impact.

True ministry, Paul says, isn't about credentials or applause. It's not even about visible success. It's about **integrity, authenticity,** and **spiritual substance**.

*"You yourselves are our letter,"* he tells the Corinthians, *"written on our hearts, known and read by everyone."*

This is **undeniable reality**: the lives transformed by the gospel are the living proof of its power. Not tablets of stone, like the old covenant. Not parchment inked by scribes. But human hearts, etched by the Spirit.

Paul names what authentic Christianity looks like:

- **Unquenchable Optimism** — even in hardship, we walk in Christ's triumph.

- **Unvarying Success** — not measured by numbers, but by faithful gospel witness.

- **Unforgettable Impact** — the aroma of Christ changes people, one way or another.

- **Unimpeachable Integrity** — we speak plainly, not peddling God's word for profit (4:2).

- **Undeniable Reality** — the Spirit writes on hearts, not stone.

You are a book, Paul says. Your life tells a story. It has authors—Christ, the Spirit, and those who ministered to you. It has a message. It bears marks not of ink, but of the transforming presence of God.

This is the glory of the new covenant—not fading like Moses' veiled face, but **ever-increasing**, as we are being transformed into Christ's likeness by the spirit of the Lord (2 Cor. 3:18).

We are **living letters**, mailed into the world, carrying grace on every page.

### "Written in Light"

Not stone, not scroll, not inked decree,
But hearts made new and minds set free.

The hand that formed the stars above
Now writes our names in sacred love.

We are the pages, scarred and blessed,
Where Spirit breathes and truth finds rest.
So let our lives declare His grace—
A letter sent from mercy's place.


## Reflections from the Road

1. What does it mean to be a "living letter" from Christ? What does your life currently communicate?

2. How does Paul's confidence in triumph (2:14) coexist with his suffering and hardship?

3. Why is integrity such a central part of gospel ministry according to this passage?

4. In what ways is the new covenant more glorious than the old? How does the Spirit write on our hearts?

5. Who are the "co-authors" of your spiritual story? Whose lives are being written on because of your ministry?

# 41

# Ministers of Reconciliation

## *2 Corinthians 5:1–21*

Paul lifts the veil in 2 Corinthians 5, offering not only comfort but cosmic clarity. He speaks not merely of death, but of **transition**. Not of an end, but of an **exchange**.

*"For we know that if the earthly tent we live in is destroyed, we have a building from God, an eternal house in heaven, not built by human hands."* (5:1)

This is not the Jewish expectation of resurrection alone, as "standing again" in bodily form. Here, Paul draws us into **timelessness** — the realm beyond clocks and calendars, the domain of God. To be absent from the body is not to wait in shadows but *to be present with the Lord*.

The physical gives way to the spiritual, the temporary to the eternal, the tent to the house. We do not become unclothed spirits, drifting and disembodied. We are **clothed anew**, fully alive, swallowed up by life itself. In that instant, **time collapses into eternity** and we are at home.

And because of this hope, Paul declares his ambition:

*"Whether we are at home in the body or away from it, we make it our aim to please Him."*

Why do we serve? Why do we speak? Why do we endure?

Three reasons:

**1. Accountability** — *For we must all appear before the judgment seat of Christ* (5:10).

**2. Urgency** — *Knowing the fear of the Lord, we persuade others* (5:11).

**3. Love** — *The love of Christ compels us* (5:14).

It is Christ's love—not ours for Him, but His for us and for the world—that drives Paul forward. That love leads to transformation. In Christ, we are **new creations**. The old has gone. The new has come.

And with this transformation comes a mission:

**God was in Christ, reconciling the world to Himself**. And He has entrusted to us the message and ministry of reconciliation.

We are not tourists in this world. We are **ambassadors** of a coming Kingdom, citizens of a realm not yet fully seen, carrying with us both the heart and the authority of our King.

And what is our message?

*"God made Him who had no sin to be sin for us, so that in Him we might become the righteousness of God."*

This is Paul at full strength. This is the gospel in radiant fullness. This is the moment where **theology becomes worship**, and **calling becomes commission**.

### "The Message We Carry"

Not clothed in might or royal garb,
We bear no sword, we wear no crown—
But mercy marks our feet with fire,
And love has pressed the message down.

He made Him sin who knew no wrong,
That we, once lost, might now belong.
So now we go with hearts made new,
Ambassadors of what is true.

**Reflections from the Road**

1. How does Paul's description of death as a transition from tent to house reframe our view of eternity?

2. Which of Paul's motivations for ministry—accountability, urgency, love—resonates most with you right now?

3. What does it mean that we are "*new creations*" in Christ? What old things in your life have passed away?

4. How do you understand your role as an ambassador of Christ? What does that mean in daily terms?

5. In what ways does the message of reconciliation speak to the divisions and brokenness of today's world?


# 42

# The Grace of Giving

## *2 Corinthians 8–9*


When Paul speaks of giving, he doesn't start with obligation. He starts with **grace**.

*"We want you to know about the grace that God has given the Macedonian churches..."* (8:1)

These were not wealthy believers. The Macedonians were poor, persecuted, worn thin. But they gave—not from abundance, but from *abandonment*. They gave themselves first to the Lord, and then they gave to the needs of others with joy, generosity, and urgency.

Paul holds them up not to shame the Corinthians, but to inspire them. He knew the Corinthians had promised to help with the offering for the struggling church in Jerusalem. But promises fade. Enthusiasm wanes. And now, Paul writes to rekindle the fire.

What follows is one of the most beautiful teachings on generosity in all of Scripture:

- Giving is a **grace**, not a transaction.

- It should be **willing**, not coerced.

- It should be **proportional**, but also **sacrificial**.

- It should reflect **cheerfulness**, not compulsion.

*"Each of you should give what you have decided in your heart to give, not reluctantly or under compulsion, for God loves a cheerful giver."* (9:7)

But the heart of it is this:

*"For you know the grace of our Lord Jesus Christ, that though He was rich, yet for your sake He became poor, so that you through His poverty might become rich."* (8:9)

Christian giving flows from **Christ's self-giving**.

We give because He gave. We sow because He has promised a harvest. And when we give joyfully, needs are met, thanksgiving overflows, and God is glorified.

Paul isn't just raising money. He's cultivating a people shaped by grace—a people who, like the widow at the temple and the Macedonians in their affliction, understand that **true generosity doesn't wait for excess. It flows from love.**

## "Out of Poverty, Overflow"

Not from fullness did they give,
But from ache and want and grace—
The kind of love that measures not,
But pours with open face.

The widow's coins, the Savior's cross,
The Macedonian song—
Such gifts the world will call too small,
But heaven names them strong.


## Reflections from the Road

1. Why do you think Paul highlighted the Macedonian churches as an example to the Corinthians?

2. How does giving reflect not just obedience, but transformation?

3. In what ways does your giving mirror Christ's self-giving love?

4. What is the difference between giving from abundance and giving from grace?

5. How might you approach generosity differently if you saw it as a form of worship and trust?

# 43

# Glory in Weakness

## *2 Corinthians 11:16–12:10*

Paul never wanted to boast.

But Corinth forced his hand. False apostles had crept in, flaunting credentials, showmanship, and status. They questioned Paul's authority, mocked his unimpressive appearance, and belittled his suffering. The church he had poured his life into was now chasing spiritual celebrities.

So Paul responds—not with polished accolades, but with a raw, paradoxical defense:

*"I am more... in labors, in prisons, in beatings, in sleepless nights, in hunger, in shipwrecks, in dangers."*

It reads like a litany of trauma. But Paul is flipping the script. He redefines apostolic authority not by how much he has achieved, but by how much he has endured for Christ.

Then he does something even stranger: he shares a mystical vision. Fourteen years earlier, he was caught up into the third heaven. Whether in the body or out, he doesn't know. He heard things he cannot even repeat.

But even that moment of glory is overshadowed by what came next:

*"To keep me from becoming conceited, there was given me a thorn in the flesh... a messenger of Satan to torment me."*

Three times he pleaded with the Lord to take it away. But the answer came, not in removal, but in revelation: *"My grace is sufficient for you, for My power is made perfect in weakness."*

And so Paul boasts. Not in visions, not in miracles, not in triumphs. But in weakness.

This is where authority is earned. Not on stages, but in scars. Not by platform, but by perseverance. This is Paul at his most honest, most human, and most holy.

He doesn't ask to be admired. He asks to be trusted—not because he is strong, but because **Christ is**.

## "The Thorn and the Crown"

Not by strength did he ascend,
Nor did glory make him whole.
It was the thorn that taught him grace,
The wound that shaped his soul.

So now he boasts not in his rise,
But in the falls he bore.
For power rests not on the proud,
But lives where hearts are poor.

## Reflections from the Road

1. Why do you think Paul chose to defend his apostleship by sharing weakness instead of strength?

2. How does Paul's *"thorn in the flesh"* shape your understanding of unanswered prayer?

3. What kind of spiritual authority does suffering produce?

4. In what areas of your life have you seen God's power made perfect in your weakness?

5. How might you rethink leadership or influence in light of Paul's example here?

# 44

# Eyes Toward the Horizon

## *Acts 19:21–22*

The gospel had shaken Ephesus.

Miracles multiplied.
Idols fell.
Lives changed.

And still, Paul knew—the mission was not finished.

The Spirit stirred within him a restless longing:
not for more accolades,
not for safer ground,
but for **greater horizons**.

"*After I have been there, I must also see Rome.*" (Acts 19:21)

It was no passing thought.
It was a fire kindled by the Spirit of God Himself.

Paul had planted seeds in Asia Minor.
He had strengthened churches across Macedonia and Greece.

But the gospel must go farther.

The center of empire—the heart of the world's power—awaited.

*Rome.*

And beyond Rome, Paul dreamed of Spain—the farthest edge of the known world.

The apostle who once wreaked havoc on the church now burned to carry Christ's name to the ends of the earth.

## Strategic Movements Begin

Sensing the time to move, Paul acted decisively:

- He sent **Timothy and Erastus** ahead into Macedonia—to encourage, to prepare, to sow peace where he would soon follow (Acts 19:22).

- He himself remained in Ephesus *for a little while longer*, knowing the work there still needed sealing.

- He held both realities in tension: **present faithfulness** and **future readiness**.

Paul was not a man who coasted.
He was a man always reaching forward,
always pushing the borders of the Kingdom outward,
always willing to go where Christ was not yet named.


## The Vision that Drives the Church

Paul's eyes toward the horizon remind us:

- The gospel is not just for our hometowns; it is for every nation, every people, every corner of the earth.

- Comfort and contentment are the enemies of mission.

- There is always a farther shore, a darker stronghold, a soul still waiting for the light.

To follow Christ is to live with forward motion,
forward hope,
forward faith.

*"I press on toward the goal for the prize of the upward call of God in Christ Jesus"* (Philippians 3:14)

Paul's heartbeat must become ours.

## "The Farther Shore"

The lamp he bore still burned and bled,
From city stones to ocean's bed—
Yet still he dreamed, and still he prayed,
For fields where gospel seeds were laid.

Not empire's crown, nor laureled fame,
But only Christ's exalted Name—
And when he saw horizon's door,
He raised his heart to go once more.


## Reflections from the Road

1. What does Paul's longing to reach Rome and beyond teach us about the expansive nature of the gospel?

2. How can we balance being faithful in the present with readiness for the new assignments God may give?

3. Where might God be stirring you to lift your eyes—to see new fields of influence, new souls to reach?

4. What "comfort zones" might need to be surrendered so that the Kingdom can advance through your life?

5. How can your church or community live more intentionally with "eyes toward the horizon"?

---

*The collision of Kingdom and culture.*
*The idols that tremble when Truth walks among them.*
*The unseen warfare made visible.*

---

# 45

# When Idols Tremble

*Acts 19:23–41*

The gospel is never neutral.

It does not slip quietly into a city.
It confronts.
It challenges.
It changes.

And those who profit from darkness always notice.

## The Firestorm Begins

Demetrius, a silversmith of Ephesus, gathered his fellow craftsmen.

Their livelihood was under threat.

The Temple of Artemis towered over the city,
its fame and fortune a source of civic pride—and personal wealth.
The making of silver shrines, little idols of the goddess,
was a booming trade.

But now, pilgrims were hesitating.
Shrines were gathering dust.
The name of Jesus was on lips once devoted to Artemis.

Demetrius fanned the flames:

*"This Paul has persuaded and turned away many people, saying that
gods made with hands are not gods at all!"* (Acts 19:26)

The crowd ignited.

With fury in their voices and fear in their hearts,

they flooded into the massive theater, shouting:

*"Great is Artemis of the Ephesians!"*

For two hours, their cries echoed off the stone walls.

Two hours—of chaos, confusion, and collective rage.

## The Gospel Disrupts Economies and Empires

Make no mistake:
The gospel does not merely touch private hearts.
It upends public idols.

- When lives are changed, economies built on sin falter.

- When truth is proclaimed, cultural myths crack.

- When Christ reigns in hearts, earthly powers tremble on their thrones.

The riot in Ephesus was not just about Artemis.
It was about **what happens when the true God confronts false ones.**

And the battle was fierce.

## Calm in the Storm

Paul, ever fearless, wanted to go into the theater and address the mob.
The believers restrained him.
Even city officials who respected Paul urged him not to risk his life.

Finally, the city clerk calmed the uproar,
reminding the crowd that lawful means, not riots, must address grievances.

Slowly, the mob dispersed.

But the message had already been carved into the heart of Ephesus:

The gods made by human hands are powerless.
Only the living Christ reigns.

## "The Shaking of the Shrine"

They forged their gods with skill and flame,
They sold their hope in Artemis' name—
Yet when the Nazarene was sung,
Their temples cracked, their idols clung.

For Truth had come with Spirit's breath,
And idols wept before their death—
The Maker's voice, the pilgrim's plea,
"Great is the Lord of liberty."

## Reflections from the Road

1. Why does true gospel proclamation often provoke strong reactions from cultural and economic powers?

2. How should we respond when our faithful witness causes opposition or disruption?

3. What idols—personal, political, cultural—still tremble at the true lordship of Jesus today?

4. How can we be both bold like Paul and wise like the believers who counseled him in this moment?

5. In what areas of your life or ministry is God calling you to confront idols with truth and courage?

# 46

# The Long Road of Strengthening

## *Acts 20:1–6*

The riot had faded.
The dust of Ephesus settled behind him.
But the fire within Paul burned hotter still.

He was not a man easily content.
Not a man who planted a few seeds and moved on.
He was a frontiersman of faith—
always reaching for the next horizon,
always fortifying what had been won.

### Strengthen What Has Been Planted

Leaving Ephesus, Paul moved northward through Macedonia—
Philippi, Thessalonica, Berea.

Everywhere he went, he strengthened the churches,
reaffirmed the gospel,
comforted hearts,
anchored faith.

He was not just a preacher.
He was a builder—
laying foundations that would outlive him.

In Greece (likely Corinth), he wintered—
three quiet months of ministry, prayer, and writing.

There, with storms battering the Aegean Sea,
Paul penned the letter to the Romans.

A letter for a city he had not yet seen,
but one that burned in his vision.

"*I am eager to preach the gospel to you also who are in Rome.*" (Romans 1:15)

And beyond Rome—Spain.
The ends of the earth, as they knew it.

## A Strategy of Strength and Reach

Paul's movements were not random.

He strengthened the churches to ensure the gospel would endure.
He cast vision beyond the known fields, to new frontiers.
He poured out encouragement in the present—
while dreaming of the harvests to come.

This was gospel stewardship:

- Faithful in what God had already given,

- Eager for the fields not yet sown.

## Setbacks and Redirections

A plot against Paul's life emerged as he prepared to sail from Greece to Syria.
Quiet threats, deadly intentions.

So Paul shifted again.
He returned north by land through Macedonia,
gathering companions, preparing hearts,
and setting his face, slowly, toward Jerusalem.

Not all journeys are straight.
But when the steps are guided by the Spirit,
even the detours carry destiny.

## "Roads of Iron, Roads of Hope"

The dust clung thick to sandaled feet,
Yet still he walked the broken street—
Strength to the weary, light to the torn,
A farmer of hope where hearts were worn.

The sea's wild winds could not deter,
Nor threats of swords, nor whispered stir—
He strengthened all, yet sought still more,
With dreams that reached a farther shore.


## Reflections from the Road

1. Why is strengthening existing believers just as important as reaching new ones?

2. How does Paul's vision for Rome and Spain inspire a long view of gospel mission?

3. What does Paul's willingness to shift plans show us about Spirit-led flexibility?

4. In your life, where might God be calling you both to strengthen what already exists *and* prepare for a greater horizon?

5. How can we cultivate a faith that is both grounded and reaching?


As Paul wintered in Greece, his eyes turned west—and his pen gave rise to the greatest theological vision the church would ever receive.

# 47

## The Gospel's Grand Cathedral

### *An Orientation to Romans*

When Paul wrote to the Romans, he wasn't responding to a crisis. He wasn't defending himself against rivals, rebuking false teachers, or correcting immorality. He was **laying a foundation**—the most expansive and exalted foundation in all of Christian Scripture.

Written during a winter stay in Greece (Acts 20:3), this epistle was more than correspondence. It was Paul's *magnum opus*—his missionary support letter, theological manifesto, pastoral appeal, and spiritual autobiography, all at once. He was planning to go west, beyond the familiar terrain of Asia Minor, all the way to Spain. And to get there, he needed a new base. Rome—capital of the empire and home to a strong, if divided, church—was the ideal sending center.

Its reputation likely reached Paul through friends like **Aquila and Priscilla**, Roman natives who knew its spiritual terrain.
Even before that, the church had likely been seeded at Pentecost—when Jews from Rome stood among the crowd at the birth of the church, returning home with hearts set ablaze by the gospel.
Rome was no ordinary congregation. It was the **First Church of the Empire**—poised to shape the future of the faith.

But Paul had never been to Rome. And among some Jewish believers, rumors about Paul's law-free gospel had stirred concern—he knew he would need to earn their trust.

So, he introduces himself. Not by résumé or reputation, but by laying out the **gospel he preaches**—and the **vision he carries**. What emerges is not just a letter, but a **cathedral of doctrine and grace**, structured with precision and pulsing with power.

The gospel, Paul insists, is not a new religion or a revised Judaism. It is the revelation of God's righteousness offered to all—**Jew and Gentile alike**—through the faithfulness of Jesus Christ. Romans is a universal declaration. A unity appeal. A call to mission. A defense of grace. A blueprint for the new humanity.

That's why we will walk through Romans in three great movements:

**Chapters 1–8: The Gospel According to Paul**
The human condition, justification by faith, life in the Spirit. A towering exposition of grace and glory.

**Chapters 9–11: God's Plan for Inclusion**
The fate of Israel, the mystery of mercy, and the wideness of God's redemptive vision for all peoples.

**Chapters 12–16: The Ethics of the Kingdom**
Transformed lives, surrendered wills, Spirit-shaped relationships. The gospel lived out in community.

Romans is a masterpiece—not for ivory towers, but for real churches with real divisions and real dreams. And behind it all is a man forged by grace, convinced of his calling, and determined to carry Christ to the ends of the earth.

We are not standing at the base of a hill.
We are beginning an ascent up **the Everest of Christian thought**.


**"Foundation of Fire"**

Not written in haste, nor tossed to the breeze,
But shaped with a fire that bends hearts to their knees.
Stone upon stone, word upon word,
The clearest good news the world ever heard.

No palace, no temple, no place built by men—

But truth as a mountain, unshaken since then.
Come climb, come listen, come stand and believe,
The grace of our God still waits to receive.


**Reflections from the Road**

1. Why do you think Paul spent so much time laying out his gospel to a church he had never visited?

2. How might understanding the historical and missionary background of Romans affect the way we read it?

3. What does it mean to think of Romans as a "cathedral of doctrine"? How does that image help us approach it?

4. In what ways do you see unity—as between Jews and Gentiles—as a core theme of the letter?

5. As we prepare to explore Romans, what are you personally hoping to better understand or apply?


# 48

# The Gospel According to Paul

## *Romans 1–8*


Paul opens Romans not with sentiment, but with **summons**:

*"Paul, a servant of Christ Jesus, called to be an apostle, set apart for the gospel of God..."*

This is no casual greeting. It is a trumpet blast. The gospel he proclaims is not of human origin. It is God's initiative, God's righteous-ness, God's power—and it is for all who believe.

Paul lays it out with unmatched clarity. Romans 1 through 8 is nothing less than **the gospel according to Paul**.

He begins with the human condition: all have sinned. Whether pagan or religious, moralist or rebel, no one is righteous. The wrath of God is revealed against all ungodliness because humanity has suppressed the truth, exchanged glory for lies, and fallen short of God's design. The good news begins with bad news—all choose to sin. We rebel against God's rule, descending into darkness and death.

But into this darkness, a light has dawned:

*"But now, apart from the law, the righteousness of God has been revealed..."*

Here is the heart of it all:

- **Justification by faith** through the redemptive work of Christ.

- **Peace with God** through the blood of the cross.

A new status, a new life, and a new identity.
Paul anchors his argument in Abraham—the father of faith, not by law, but by promise. And he explains the cascading effect of grace:

*"Where sin increased, grace abounded all the more."*

But grace is not license. <u>Those who are in Christ have died with Him</u> and now live by the Spirit. Sin no longer has dominion. The law cannot condemn. The Spirit testifies that we are children of God.

Romans 8 rises like a peak above the rest:

*"There is therefore now no condemnation for those who are in Christ Jesus."*

From foreknowledge to glorification, from suffering to victory, from groaning to hope, Paul declares that nothing—not life, not death, not height, depth, angels or demons—can separate us from the love of God in Christ.

This is more than theology. This is **freedom**, **identity**, and **invitation**.

Romans 1–8 is the **deep well of the gospel**, and Paul invites us to draw from it again and again.

## "No Condemnation"

From wrath revealed to mercy poured,
From Adam's fall to Heaven's door—
He writes a song of love and grace,
Where sinners find a Savior's face.

The law condemned, but could not save,
The cross has made a deeper way.
And now in Christ, the chains are gone,
The cry of freedom is our song.

## Reflections from the Road

1. Why does Paul spend so much time building the case that all have sinned before he announces the good news?

2. What is the difference between righteousness earned by law and righteousness given by faith?

3. How does Romans 6 challenge the idea that grace gives permission to sin?

4. What comfort do you draw from the promises in Romans 8?

5. How would you explain "justification" to someone unfamiliar with Christian vocabulary?

# 49

# God's Plan for Inclusion

## *Romans 9–11*

At the height of his gospel declaration, Paul turns to a painful question:

"What about Israel?"

If God has made salvation available to all through Christ, then what of His ancient covenant people? Has His promise failed? Has Israel been cast aside?

Paul answers with deep sorrow and theological precision.

*"I could wish myself accursed and cut off from Christ for the sake of my brothers..."*

This is not cold logic. It is the cry of a man torn between his love for Israel and his revelation of the gospel.

Paul walks a fine line:

- He affirms that **God's word has not failed**.

- He shows that **not all Israel are Israel** — but the children of the promise.

He highlights God's sovereign mercy: *"I will have mercy on whom I have mercy."*
But this is no rejection story. It is a **mystery of inclusion**.

Israel stumbled, yes—but only that the Gentiles might come in. The Gentiles were grafted in—yes—but only to provoke Israel to return.

Paul calls it a holy tension, a divine strategy, a mercy-soaked plan unfolding over time. And at the end, he writes:

*"God has bound all over to disobedience so that He may have mercy on them all."*

The end of Romans 11 is not a conclusion. It is a doxology:

*"Oh, the depth of the riches of the wisdom and knowledge of God!"*

This is the God who weaves rebellion into redemption, who takes what was broken and turns it into blessing. The gospel is not about exclusion. It is about **expansion**.

And Paul, the apostle to the Gentiles, says: *This has always been the plan.*

### "Grafted"

They stumbled first, we entered next,
But neither was the end.
The Root remains, the branches grow,
And mercy will not bend.

He binds us all, He calls us all,
From wrath and works and pride—
That none may boast, but all may kneel,
Where grace and truth abide.

### Reflections from the Road

1. How does Paul's sorrow for Israel shape the tone of Romans 9–11?

2. What does it mean that not all descended from Israel are part of true Israel?

3. How do these chapters challenge ideas of exclusion or spiritual elitism?

4. Why is the metaphor of the olive tree (Romans 11) so powerful?

5. What does Paul's doxology at the end of Romans 11 say about our response to God's mysterious plan?

# 50

# The Ethics of the Kingdom

## *Romans 12–16*

Having scaled the theological heights of God's mercy, Paul comes down to earth with a single, piercing word:

*"Therefore..."*

In view of all that God has done—His grace, His righteousness, His redemptive plan—how should we then live?

Romans 12–16 answers that question. This is **the gospel embodied.** The community formed by grace must now live in a way that reflects the very character of Christ.

*"Do not be conformed to this world, but be transformed by the renewing of your mind."*

Paul calls the church to live differently:

- To offer themselves as living sacrifices.

- To think soberly about their gifts and to use them for the good of the body.

- To love sincerely, cling to what is good, and bless those who persecute.

Here we find the most beautiful and practical vision of Spirit-filled community:

- Rejoicing with those who rejoice.

- Weeping with those who weep.

- Living in harmony, humility, and peace.

But Paul goes even further:

- Submit to governing authorities.

- Owe no one anything, except to love.

- Clothe yourselves with the Lord Jesus Christ.

These are not rules. They are **reflections** of a transformed life—the marks of a new people shaped not by empire or culture, but by the cross and the resurrection.

Paul closes by addressing real divisions in the church. Jewish and Gentile believers struggled over matters of conscience: food, holy days, customs. Paul urges patience, understanding, and unity:

*"Let us not pass judgment on one another... Let us pursue what makes for peace and mutual upbuilding."*

In the Kingdom, the strong bear with the weak, and all belong to one Lord.

And finally, in chapter 16, Paul greets believers by name. The theology that began in glory ends in **real relationships**. This is not abstract doctrine. It is the **living, breathing Body of Christ**.

This is how the Kingdom looks when it walks around in flesh and blood.

## "A People Set Apart"

Not pressed into the world's old mold,
But shaped by hands of grace,
They walk in love, they speak in peace,
They shine in every place.

Their minds renewed, their hearts made clean,
Their gifts no longer stored—
They live not for themselves alone,
But for the risen Lord.

## Reflections from the Road

1. What does it mean to be a *"living sacrifice"* in your daily life?

2. How does Romans 12 challenge both individualism and self-promotion?

3. Why is love described as the only ongoing debt we owe?

4. How can Christians handle differences of opinion and practice without division?

5. What picture of the church do you see in Paul's personal greetings in Romans 16?

# 51

# Light in the Upper Room

## *Acts 20:7–12*

It was the first day of the week—Sunday—a new rhythm taking root
among the followers of Jesus.

Work had filled their daylight hours.
Slaves, craftsmen, merchants—
they labored as the world labored.

But as dusk fell and torches sputtered to life,
they gathered.

Not in grandeur.
Not in leisure.

In an upper room, crowded and dim,
with lamps smoking in the heavy night air,
they came hungry.

Hungry for the Bread of Life.


## One Last Night

Paul knew this might be his last time among them.

He spoke late into the night, weaving Scripture, memory, and hope
into every word.

The room grew stuffy.
The hours dragged on.

And one young man, perched precariously on a windowsill,
could not fight the weight of exhaustion.

Eutychus drifted into sleep—
and tumbled three stories to the ground below.


## Death Interrupted

The gathering rushed down in horror.
Eutychus was dead.

But Paul, the bearer of resurrection news,
knelt beside him.

He embraced the lifeless body—
and life returned.

*"Do not be alarmed,"* Paul said,
*"for his life is in him."* (Acts 20:10)


## The Unquenchable Hunger

They returned to the upper room.
They broke bread.
They continued speaking—until dawn.

Why?

Because when the Word burns,
no night is too long, no hunger too small, no fatigue too deep.

The early church was not built by convenience.
It was built by holy hunger—
the thirst to hear and follow Christ no matter the cost.


## A God of Mercy

Eutychus reminds us:

God does not despise our frailty.
He does not scoff at our weariness.

He meets us in it—
revives us, restores us,
and invites us back into the feast.

## "Lamps Against the Night"

The lamps burned low, the eyelids fell,
The Word still soared, the stories swelled—
A crash, a cry, a tear, a prayer,
And Life breathed hope into the air.

They broke the bread, they sang the psalm,
They found in Christ their strength, their calm—
And though the night was worn and long,
The morning found them filled with song.

## Reflections from the Road

1. What does the gathering at Troas teach us about the priorities and hunger of the early church?

2. How does God's response to Eutychus' fall reflect His mercy toward our human frailty?

3. Why is it important to gather—even when inconvenient, uncomfortable, or costly?

4. Where in your life is God calling you to press deeper into His Word, despite weariness or distraction?

5. What would it look like for your church or small group to have this kind of holy hunger today?

# 52

# Tears on the Shore

*Acts 20:17–38*

The sea breeze carried a hint of salt and sorrow.

On the shore at Miletus, Paul stood among men he had loved,
taught, and bled with—
the elders of the church at Ephesus.

He had called them to meet him here,
too pressed by time to return to the city itself,
but unwilling to slip away without a final word.


## A Shepherd's Final Charge

Paul spoke not as a commander, but as a shepherd.

*"You know how I lived the whole time I was with you,"* he began.
Not merely how he preached—how he *lived*.
With humility.
With tears.
With perseverance through trials.

He reminded them:

• He had proclaimed the whole counsel of God—holding nothing
back.

• He had ministered both publicly and house to house.

• He had warned, pleaded, and taught with unwavering faithfulness.

Now, bound by the Spirit,
he was heading toward Jerusalem—
and beyond that, uncertainty, suffering, and chains.


## The Shape of True Leadership

Paul charged them:

- **Shepherd the flock** over which the Holy Spirit had made them overseers.

- **Guard the church of God**, bought with the blood of Christ.

- **Be watchful**, for fierce wolves would arise—even from among their own ranks.

He used no grand titles.
No hierarchical trappings.

**Elder (*presbuteros*).**
**Overseer (*episkopos*).**
**Shepherd (*poimen*).**

Different words, one calling:
To love, to protect, to feed the people of God.

The early church was not built on empire, but on **family**.
Not on career paths, but on **calling**.
Not on control, but on **care**.


## The Weight of Departure

Paul knelt with them in prayer.
Tears flowed freely.

They embraced him, sorrowing most over his final words:

*"You will never see my face again."*

There, on the rocky shore,
they clung not to positions, not to programs,
but to one another—
to the bond Christ Himself had forged between them.

This was the church at its truest:
relational, Spirit-led, anchored in love.

And the waves whispered their amen.

## "The Last Embrace"

Upon the shore where salt winds sighed,
The shepherd spoke, the brethren cried—
Not for a throne, nor for a name,
But for the love through which he came.

No empire's gold, no titles crowned,
But hearts in sacred calling bound—
And tears, like tides, their parting sealed,
Until the final trump revealed.

## Reflections from the Road

1. What qualities marked Paul's leadership among the Ephesians?

2. How does the early church's model of leadership challenge our modern assumptions about power and structure?

3. What does it mean to shepherd the flock of God with humility and vigilance today?

4. How do we prepare those we love and lead for the day when we are no longer there?

5. In what ways are you being called to a deeper stewardship of the people and opportunities God has entrusted to you?

# Interlude

## *The Shepherds and the Sovereigns*

The sea lapped against the stones at Miletus.

On a rugged shore, Paul wept with the elders of Ephesus,
men he had discipled, prayed with, suffered alongside.

There were no golden crowns.
No embroidered robes.
No miters, no scepters, no crimson processions.

Only tear-streaked faces.
Only calloused hands gripping shoulders in a last embrace.
Only the Kingdom of God in its rawest, realest form.

### The Simplicity of the Shepherds

They were elders.
Overseers.
Shepherds.

Three words for one calling:

- To guard the flock.

- To feed the sheep.

- To protect the vulnerable.

- To serve, not to be served.

They were chosen not for prestige, but for proven faith.
They were called not to rule, but to watch over.
They wore not crowns, but burdens.

This was the church as Christ intended it:

A Body, not a bureaucracy.
A family, not an empire.


## The Drift Begins

But Paul knew.

"*After my departure,*" he warned,
"*savage wolves will come in among you, not sparing the flock.*"

Some of the wolves would come from without.
Some from within.

History would prove it:

- Within three centuries, the church would be allied with earthly power.

- Bishops would become city rulers.

- Wealth and politics would infiltrate pulpits.

- Titles would multiply as humility withered.

Robes and miters would rise as dusty cloaks were laid aside.
The Body would still survive—
but buried under layers of worldly grandeur.

The Bride would still exist—
but often hidden beneath the trappings of empire.


## Still the Kingdom Endures

Yet not all would be lost.

Across the centuries, across the continents,
in caves and kitchens, in fields and prisons,
the true church would persist:

- Where hearts stayed simple.

- Where leadership remained servant-hearted.

- Where Christ—not Caesar, not Constantine, not clerical titles—
was Lord.

- Where the Shepherd's voice still called,
there the sheep would still gather.

Small bands, secret gatherings, persecuted witnesses—
but always alive, always burning.

## The Choice Before Us

Each generation faces the same choice:

Will we walk the dusty shore with Paul,
the road of the cross, the burden of the shepherd?

Or will we chase the grand procession,
the banners, the palaces, the applause?

The shepherds still rise.
The sovereigns still beckon.

The path is still before us.

## "The Silent Bells"

No marble dome, no golden chime,
No thundered creed, no measured time—
But whispered prayers where shadows fall,
And broken feet that heed the call.

The sovereign's towers touch the skies,
The Shepherd's flock in silence lies—
And through the noise, His voice still swells:
*"My Kingdom moves by silent bells."*

### Reflections from the Road

1. How does Paul's farewell to the Ephesian elders illustrate the heart of true spiritual leadership?

2. What are the dangers of aligning the church too closely with political or worldly power?

3. How can today's church recapture the Spirit-led simplicity and relational strength of the early believers?

4. In your own leadership or ministry, are you leaning more toward the shepherd's path—or the sovereign's lure?

5. What steps can you take to embody and encourage Spirit-led, Christ-centered community in your context?

# 53

# Chains and Chances

## From Jerusalem to Caesarea

### *Acts 21–23*

The warnings were clear.

Prophets bound themselves in belts.
Friends pleaded with tearful eyes.
Brothers and sisters begged him not to go.

But Paul set his face toward Jerusalem.

Not recklessly.

Not naively.

He went knowing that the path of obedience would be paved with chains.

## A City on Edge

The city seethed with tension.
Old hatreds had not cooled.
New resentments festered.

When Paul entered the temple, it was as if a match had been struck.
Rumors flared. Accusations spread.
*"This is the man who teaches against our people, our law, and this place!"*

A mob erupted.
Paul was dragged out.
The temple gates slammed shut behind him.

It was not the prayers of the devout that spared Paul's life that day—
it was the iron grip of Roman authority.

Soldiers seized him from the fray,
lifting him above the violence.

Bound in chains,
he asked for one thing:
*"Let me speak."*

## The Defense of a Man Unashamed

On the temple steps, with blood still pounding in the air,
Paul gave his defense:

- His Jewish heritage.

- His zeal as a Pharisee.

- His encounter with Christ.

- His commission to the Gentiles.

But when he spoke of the nations,
the fury reignited.

The crowd erupted anew,
and the Romans pulled him into the barracks—
not out of sympathy, but to scourge and interrogate.

Paul, ever the strategist, revealed his Roman citizenship.
The whip was lowered.
The process shifted.


## The Unseen Hand of God

In the quiet of captivity, the Lord appeared to him:

*"Take courage. As you have testified about Me in Jerusalem, so you must also testify in Rome."* (Acts 23:11)

Jerusalem was not the end.

The chains were not the defeat.

They were the bridge.


## A Conspiracy in the Shadows

Forty men bound themselves with an oath.
They would not eat or drink until Paul was dead.

But God's providence worked through the ordinary:

- Paul's nephew overheard the plot.

- The young man warned the Roman commander.

Action was taken swiftly.

Two hundred soldiers, seventy horsemen, and two hundred spear-
men—a full military escort—protected the apostle as he was moved
by night to Caesarea.

Hidden epistles, hidden plots, hidden hands—
but God's purposes moved in open power.


## A Letter and a New Stage

The Roman commander, Claudius Lysias, penned a letter: a hidden
epistle, preserving Paul's innocence in official Roman records.

Paul was delivered to Felix, governor of Judea,
and placed under guard in Herod's Praetorium.

The scene shifted.
The pace quickened.

From the seething streets of Jerusalem
to the polished stones of Caesarea, step by step,
the gospel was moving toward the heart of the empire.

Chains could not stop it.
Plots could not derail it.
Politics could not contain it.

God was writing a story larger than any court, larger than any king.

And Paul—bound but unbroken—was still the pen in His hand.


## "The Chain Was the Bridge"

They thought the chain would seal his fate,
They thought the gate would close—
But every link, by heaven's craft,
Became the path God chose.

No plot, no blade, no whispered scheme

Could snuff the Spirit's flame—
For bound or free, in shade or sun,
Paul bore the Master's name.

### Reflections from the Road

1. How does Paul's courage in Jerusalem challenge our understanding of faithfulness in hostile environments?

2. What does God's hidden providence through ordinary means (e.g., Paul's nephew) teach us about trusting Him?

3. How do Paul's chains become a symbol of unstoppable mission rather than defeat?

4. Are there "chains" in your life right now that God might be using as bridges to a greater purpose?

5. How can you cultivate courage to speak the gospel, even when the environment is hostile or uncertain?

# 54

# Almost Persuaded: The Gospel on Trial

## *Acts 24–26*

The halls of power echoed with polished words and political games.

Paul, in chains, stood before governors and kings.
But he was no victim.
He was the freest man in the room.

## Felix: Justice for Sale

Before the Roman governor Felix,
Paul laid out the gospel with clarity and courage:

- Faith in Christ.

- Righteousness, self-control, and the coming judgment.

Felix trembled.

But trembling is not the same as repentance.

He sent Paul away, hoping for a bribe,
keeping him confined for two long years—
not because he was guilty,
but because justice was a commodity to be bartered.

Paul waited.
But Paul did not waste.


## Festus: Confusion and Expediency

When Felix was succeeded by Festus,
Paul again found himself explaining the hope of the resurrection.

Festus, baffled by Jewish religious disputes,
wanted to do the Jews a favor.

But Paul had learned:

- Earthly courts are not the final judges.

- Politics bends toward expedience, not truth.

Paul played his final Roman card:
"*I appeal to Caesar!*"

The die was cast.
Rome lay ahead.

## Agrippa: The "Almost" King

Before Paul could be sent to Caesar,
King Agrippa and his sister Bernice arrived—
and Festus arranged for a hearing.

This was no backroom interrogation.

It was a spectacle:
regal robes, jeweled thrones, military tribunes—
the trappings of earthly power on full display.

But when Paul spoke,
the room shifted.

He was not the accused.
He was the ambassador.

Paul told his story again:

- His zealous beginnings.

- His blinding encounter with the risen Christ.

- His commission to proclaim light to Jews and Gentiles.

He spoke with urgency, with clarity, with heart.

Festus, unable to comprehend spiritual matters, interrupted:

*"Paul, you are out of your mind; your great learning is driving you mad!"*

Paul, steady as a mountain, replied:
*"I am not out of my mind, most excellent Festus, but I speak true and rational words."*

Then he turned to Agrippa:

*"King Agrippa, do you believe the prophets? I know you do."*

Agrippa's answer echoes across the ages:

***"Almost you persuade me to become a Christian."*** (Acts 26:28)

Almost.
The tragedy of "almost."


## The Unyielding Witness

Paul, chained but unconquered, replied:

*"I would to God that not only you but also all who hear me this day might become such as I am—except for these chains."*

He did not beg.
He did not plead for release.

He offered freedom.
True freedom.


## The Court's Verdict

The officials conferred among themselves:

*"This man could have been set free if he had not appealed to Caesar."*

But Paul did not regret it.

Freedom was not his goal.
Rome—and the gospel's advance to the heart of the empire—was.

Chains or no chains,
Paul belonged to a higher court.


## "Almost"

Almost a flame, yet cold with fear,
Almost a cry, but none to hear—
Almost a crown, but left unclaimed,
Almost a heart, but never named.

Almost a soul redeemed from loss—
But almost stands…

On the wrong side of the cross.


**Reflections from the Road**

1. What does Paul's demeanor before Felix, Festus, and Agrippa teach us about witnessing under pressure?

2. Why is "almost persuaded" such a devastating place to remain?

3. How does Paul's steady vision of Rome—and beyond—challenge us to keep a Kingdom-centered focus?

4. Are there areas in your life where you are lingering in "almost" rather than stepping fully into faith and obedience?

5. How can we, like Paul, see our circumstances (even trials or hardships) as platforms for proclaiming Christ?


# 55

# The Storm and the Steadfast Heart

*Acts 27*


The winds were against them from the start.

The ship strained against the sea,
and so did the men—
struggling, second-guessing, fearing.

Paul, a prisoner in chains, was not at the helm.

But he held something more powerful than the rudder:
the Word of the living God.


## When Wisdom Was Ignored

Paul warned them:
*"Men, I perceive that the voyage will end in disaster..."*

But the captain trusted his charts.
The owner trusted his profit.
The centurion trusted the professionals.

And so they sailed into the teeth of the storm.

Sometimes the world sails straight toward ruin,
ignoring the voice of truth in its midst.


## When Hope Was Lost

For fourteen days,
the ship was driven mercilessly by the wind.

- Food was abandoned.

- Cargo was thrown overboard.

Despair crept in like the rising tide.
Luke writes with brutal honesty:

*"All hope of our being saved was at last abandoned."* (Acts 27:20)

Except in one man.

Paul stood, unshaken:

*"Take heart... for there will be no loss of life among you, but only of the ship."* (27:22)

How did he know?

Because in the night, a messenger had stood beside him:

*"Do not be afraid, Paul. You must stand before Caesar. And behold, God has granted you all those who sail with you."* (27:24)

Chains could not bind the promises of God.


## When Leadership Was Spirit-Born

In a ship without compass,
Paul became the steady hand.

- He counseled prudence.

- He urged courage.

- He gave thanks to God in front of unbelievers.

- He blessed broken bread when the sailors could barely lift their heads.

Leadership was not seized.
It was earned—by steadfastness under pressure.

Paul didn't steer the ship to Malta.
The wind and waves did.

But Paul steered the souls toward hope.


## When the Ship Was Lost, the Mission Was Not

The ship shattered on unseen reefs.
Cold waves swallowed wood and cargo alike.

But every man reached the shore alive—
just as God had said.

The storm wrecked their vessel,
but it did not wreck the voyage.

Because the voyage was never about the ship.

It was about the Kingdom.

And the Kingdom advances through storms,
through wrecks, through nights when hope seems lost—

**if someone will stand steadfast in the gale.**


### "The Calm Within the Gale"

The winds may howl, the timbers break,
The stars may hide, the strong may quake—
But he who holds the Master's hand
Will find his footing on shifting sand.

For chains are light and storms are small,
When Christ, the Captain, commands them all.


### Reflections from the Road

1. What can Paul's calmness during the storm teach us about leadership in chaotic times?

2. Why is spiritual steadiness more important than worldly status in moments of crisis?

3. How does the shipwreck reveal the difference between what we cling to and what truly matters?

4. Are you prepared to lead others toward hope when the storm breaks?

5. What storms in your life might be opportunities to bear witness to the unwavering promises of God?

# 56

## *Unhinderedly*

## The Triumph of the Gospel

### *Acts 28*

They came to him in chains.

Some came as brothers,
bringing encouragement,
blessing the weary apostle with their presence.

Some came as skeptics,
weighing his words,
seeking a reason to dismiss the gospel he proclaimed.

But whether friend or questioner,
whether ruler or prisoner,
whether citizen or slave—
Paul welcomed them all.

The door was open.
The Word was open.
The Kingdom was moving forward.


**Two Years, A World Opened**

Under house arrest in Rome, Paul was not idle.

He taught.
He testified.
He wrote.

From the confines of rented quarters came letters that would shape the church forever:

- **Ephesians** — the glorious mystery of the Body of Christ.

- **Colossians** — the supremacy of Christ over all creation.

- **Philippians** — the joy of Christ in suffering.

- **Philemon** — the transforming power of grace in relationships.

No palace proclamation could match the impact of these prison-born words.

Rome's chains could not silence the Kingdom.


## The Gospel in the Capital of the World

Luke tells us:

*"Paul welcomed all who came to him, proclaiming the Kingdom of God and teaching about the Lord Jesus Christ with all boldness and without hindrance."* (Acts 28:30–31)

No barriers.
No apologies.
No retreat.

The gospel had reached the beating heart of the empire.

It had crossed seas, outlasted storms, out-argued philosophers, and now it stood unbowed within sight of Caesar's throne.


## Not Peter, but Paul

There is no mention of Peter in Rome in Acts.
No grand papal procession.
No founding of thrones or kingdoms.

Only a prisoner,
writing letters,
opening Scripture,
and announcing a Kingdom not of this world.

Paul, the aged apostle,
stood as a living embodiment of Christ's unstoppable gospel.


**The Last Word**

Frank Stagg was right.

In the Greek text of Acts, the last word is ***akolutos*** —
**unhinderedly**.

Luke did not end Acts with the death of Paul,
nor with a recounting of his achievements.

He ended it with the gospel,
living and moving beyond any human chain.

The story had not ended.
It was just beginning.

The gospel would move on—

- Over racial barriers.

- Over religious barriers.

- Over class and gender barriers.

- Over cultural and geographic barriers.

- Over political opposition.

- Over personal weakness.

- Over imperial might.

- Over prison walls.

Over every obstacle man could raise.
*Unhinderedly*.


## "Unhinderedly"

No sword could still the trumpet's blast,
No chain could hold the Word so vast—
No emperor's wrath, no prison wall
Could halt the call, could hush the call.

The tomb was empty, the Throne secure,
The gospel raced, steadfast and pure.
And still today it runs its course—
Unhindered by the world's brute force.


## Reflections from the Road

1. How does the image of Paul in Rome challenge our understanding of success and faithfulness?

2. In what ways is the gospel still moving "*unhinderedly*" today?

3. Where might God be calling you to proclaim the Kingdom with boldness, even in hard or confined places?

4. What "chains" in your life might God be using as a platform for His Word?

5. Will you live your days so that when your story ends, the gospel is still moving forward through you?

# Interlude

## Letters from Prison, Messages for the Church

### *Ephesians & Colossians*

Paul wrote Ephesians and Colossians from prison, but their message could not be confined. Though addressed to different churches, these letters are theological twins—distinct in tone and audience, yet united in truth. They complement each other like mirror and reflection—Ephesians celebrates the Church as Christ's Body; Colossians exalts Christ as the Head. Together, they reveal that only under Christ—and in Christ—does the Church become what it was meant to be.

But the audiences were very different.

### To the Ephesians: Old Friends, Deep Roots

Paul knew the Ephesian church intimately. He writes as a friend and founder. He had taught there for over two years (Acts 19:10), establishing a strong, Spirit-filled community in one of the empire's most influential cities. His letter to them reads like a soaring anthem of identity and purpose:

*"You are no longer foreigners and strangers, but fellow citizens with God's people and also members of his household."*

Ephesians expands on themes of unity, grace, spiritual gifting, and maturity. It casts a cosmic vision of the Church—not just as a community, but as **Christ's living Body** on earth. His tone is majestic, painting a grand vision of the Church—unified, gifted, and mature in Christ. Ephesians lifts our eyes to the cosmic plan of God. Writing with joy, Paul urges the Ephesian believers to walk in love, live by grace, stand in unity, and grow into the full stature of Christ.

187

## To the Colossians: A Church by Reputation

Paul had never visited Colossae. The church there was likely founded during his extended ministry in Ephesus. Epaphras, one of Paul's co-workers, had carried the gospel inland and now reported troubling news: the Colossians were under pressure from **false teachers** blending elements of Jewish law, Greek philosophy, mysticism, and asceticism. The heart of the teachings: a diminished view of Christ.

Paul's response is sharp and theological. He confronts:

- **Jewish legalism**: insisting Christ fulfilled the Law.
- **Mysticism and asceticism**: warning against man-made rules and self-denial as false paths to holiness.
- **Worship of angels**: rejecting spiritual hierarchies that displaced Christ
- **Philosophical dualism**: confronting the idea that physical matter is evil, and affirming the incarnation.

When confronted by this diminished view of Christ, Paul corrects that with one of the most exalted Christological declarations in Scripture: *"He is the image of the invisible God... all things were created by Him and for Him... and in Him all things hold together."*

Colossians is a call to **keep Christ central**. Paul anchors their identity in the supremacy of Jesus: not an idea, not a system, but a living Lord.

Paul's response is clear and forceful:

- Christ is not one among many; He is the image of the invisible God.
- Christ is not a created mediator; He is firstborn over all creation.
- Christ is not a stepping-stone to maturity; He is the fullness of God in bodily form.
- Christ is not merely the Church's founder; He is its Head and sustaining force.

To Ephesus, Paul builds up the Body.
To Colossae, Paul enthrones the Head.

Together, these letters proclaim:

- The Church must live in unity and maturity (*Ephesians*).
- The Church must hold fast to Christ alone (Colossians).

And though written in chains, Paul's words carry liberating power. These are not just letters of theology—they are blueprints for a Church rooted in grace, centered on Christ, and alive with purpose.

## "Bound, Yet Free"

From prison walls the letters flew,
To saints both known and yet brand new.
To one he wrote of Body grace,
To one he showed Christ's rightful place.
He penned the truth, both wide and deep,
That Christ alone the soul must keep.
No angel, rite, or rule of men—
But Christ, the First, the Last, the When.

## Reflections from the Road

1. Why is it significant that Paul wrote both letters from prison?
2. How does Paul's long relationship with Ephesus shape the tone of his letter to them?
3. What challenges in Colossae prompted such a clear defense of Christ's supremacy?
4. What modern parallels can you see to the kinds of false teachings Paul confronted?
5. How do Ephesians and Colossians together deepen your understanding of what the Church is and who Christ is?

# 57

# Many Gifts, One Body

## *A Devotional Reflection on Spiritual Gifts*

In the New Testament many images are used to help us understand the Church. The Church is compared to an army, a bride, a building, a flock, leaven, fire, branches, a family. Of all these teaching images used to help us understand the nature and function of the Church, the imagery of the human body is the most widely used image in the New Testament.

Paul uses this image to describe the Church--none is more personal or more practical—than the body. It speaks of design, of dependence, of diversity working in unity. In Ephesians, Romans, Corinthians, and Colossians, Paul returns to this metaphor again and again, helping believers understand what it means to belong—and to serve.

In the Church, no one is giftless. No one is purposeless—
*"To each one grace has been given as Christ apportioned it."* (Eph. 4:7)
*"Now you are the body of Christ and members in particular."* (1 Cor. 12:27)

We are grace-gifted. Charismatically empowered. Each believer's combination of gifts becomes their spiritual fingerprint—a unique expression of God's purpose through them.


### The Color of Calling

Think of the rainbow. Though it appears in bands of six colors, it is made from only three primaries—red, yellow, blue. (And before you turn off by a simple illustration—yes, we know that a rainbow is composed from the refraction of light wave spectrum…and if the actual rainbow doesn't work for you, think of creating a rainbow with paint.) Their combinations form the visible arc of beauty. So it is with spiritual gifts. A handful of divine colors—teaching, giving, serving, leading—blend uniquely in each life. The result? A ministry as distinct as a fingerprint, as radiant as refracted light.

## Synergy in the Spirit

When believers serve together, something remarkable happens. The effect is greater than the sum of the parts. This is synergy. One gift supports another. One believer's weakness is covered by another's strength. The Body grows—not by duplication, but by coordination. Like strands in a braided cord, our diversity becomes our strength.

## A Word for the Weary

Some may feel unnecessary—like a toe in a world of eyes and hands. But Paul rebukes such self-depreciation:
*"if the foot says, 'Because I am not a hand, I do not belong to the body,' it would not for that reason stop being part of the body."* (1 Cor. 12:15)

Others may feel self-sufficient—content to work alone. But Paul warns against that too:
*"The eye cannot say to the hand, 'I don't need you!'"* (1 Cor. 12:21)

We are not independent parts. We are interdependent. Our wholeness depends on one another.

## The Body in Motion

What does this look like in action? It looks like:

- Teachers illuminating Scripture.

- Servants meeting needs before they're spoken.

191

- Leaders charting Spirit-led paths.

- Givers supplying what others lack.

- Encouragers lifting the weary.

Every part matters. Every gift counts. Every believer has a place.

When each member contributes their part, the Body builds itself up in love. It becomes visible, vibrant, alive—Christ's presence, moving in the world.

**"The Rainbow Within"**
Three colors form the arch we see,
Yet six shine out in unity.
So gifts from God, both bold and shy,
Combine to paint His purpose high.
No hand alone, no foot ignored,
All needed in the risen Lord.
In grace we serve, in strength we grow—
Together, Christ's great Church will glow.

**Reflections from the Road**

1.What gifts has God woven together in your life to form your unique ministry?

2. Have you ever struggled with feeling unnecessary—or overly self -reliant—in the Body? How does Paul's teaching speak to that?

3. Where do you see synergy in your church—people working together in ways that multiply impact?

4. What steps can you take to better understand and use your gifts for the good of the Body?

5. How can we celebrate our differences instead of just tolerating them?

# 58

# The Body and The Head
## *Ephesians & Colossians*

No image captures the Church's relationship to Christ more profoundly than the human body. It is not an organization but an organism—living, growing, responsive. Paul weaves this image throughout his letters. In Ephesians and Colossians, it reaches full clarity.

**Christ is the Head.**
**The Church is His Body.**
This is not a metaphor of sentiment—it is a declaration of spiritual reality.

*"He is the head of the body, the church..."* (Col. 1:18)
*"From him the whole body... grows and builds itself up in love, as each part does its work."* (Eph. 4:16)

Christ is not detached from His Church. His life animates our life. His wisdom orders our movement. His Spirit directs our growth. When that connection is severed—when the Church moves without the Head—it becomes chaotic, disordered, and powerless.

Paul emphasizes two essential truths:

## 1. Christ is Supreme

The Colossians needed to be reminded that Jesus was not merely a spiritual figure among many.
He is the image of the invisible God, the Creator and Sustainer of all things. No angel, ritual, or philosophy can replace Him.
He is **first in rank, first in time, and first in authority**.

*"In him all things hold together..."* (Col. 1:17)

## 2. The Church is Unified by His Life

The Ephesians, by contrast, were urged to grow together into maturity. Christ, as Head, equips and empowers His Body through grace-gifted members who function in harmony. Leadership is not a status but a service: to equip others so that **the whole Body builds itself up in love.**

This is the mystery of synergy:

- One member cannot replace another.

- Every gift contributes to the health of the whole.

The Church flourishes not through celebrity or hierarchy, but through interdependence and shared purpose.
When Christ is truly Head—and the Church truly responsive—His will is done on earth as it is in heaven.
His compassion is made visible.
His truth is proclaimed.
His mission moves forward through ordinary people led by an extraordinary Savior.

We are not just Christ's followers.
We are His Body—moved by His mind, filled with His Spirit, living out His love.


### "The Body, the Head"
He speaks, and hands begin to move,
He sees, and hearts arise to love.
No part alone, no gift in vain—
Each pulse, each breath, a holy chain.
The Head, enthroned above all powers,
Commands the Body's living hours.
And we, though many, live as one—
The Church, His work not yet done.

### Reflections from the Road

1. What does it mean in practice for Christ to be the Head of the Church?

2. Where have you seen the Church fail to follow its Head? What were the results?

3. How does Paul's vision of interdependence reshape your view of spiritual gifts?

4. What would it look like for your local church to function fully under Christ's leadership?

5. In what ways can you personally align more closely with Christ as the Head?

# 59

# How the Body Functions
### *Ephesians 4:1–16; Colossians 1:28*

The Church is not a passive gathering.
It is a living Body—diverse in its members, unified in its calling, and moving under the direction of Christ the Head.

Paul begins not with strategy, but with character:
*"Walk in a manner worthy of the calling to which you have been called…"* (Eph. 4:1)

That walk is marked by humility, gentleness, patience, and love— virtues that guard the unity the Spirit has already created.

We are one Body, Paul says—held together by *one Spirit, one hope, one Lord, one faith, one baptism, one God and Father of all* (Eph. 4:4-6).

## Diversity Within Unity

But unity does not mean uniformity.
Within the one Body, God has woven diverse gifts—each grace-given, each essential— *"But to each one of us grace has been given as Christ apportioned it."* (Eph. 4:7)

Paul names a few roles—apostles, prophets, evangelists, and pastor-teachers—not as superior classes, but as servant leaders whose job is not to perform the ministry but to **prepare the people who do**.

The Greek word Paul uses—*katartizo*—means to mend, equip, make fully ready. It's used for restoring nets, outfitting soldiers, and furnishing craftsmen. This is the quiet, faithful task of pastoral ministry: shaping the Body to serve and grow.

This equipping leads to real outcomes:

- Unity in faith
- Knowledge of the Son of God
- Maturity in character
- Stability against falsehood
- Growth into the full stature of Christ

*"We proclaim Him, admonishing and teaching everyone with all wisdom, so that we may present everyone mature in Christ."* (Col. 1:28)

## Synergy in the Body

When each member functions properly, the Body builds itself up in love.

This is more than organization. It is **synergy**—the divine multiplication that occurs when every part contributes.

Not hierarchy. Not celebrity. Not control.

But Spirit-led, Christ-centered, Body-wide cooperation.

The hand can't replace the foot. The ear can't become the eye. Yet each part matters. Every ligament counts. And when all work together, the whole becomes far greater than the sum of its parts.

We are not spectators. We are participants.

We are each ministers—called, gifted, and placed by God for a purpose.


### "Call, Many Gifts"

Not one, but many, shaped and sent,
By grace and gifting, heaven-bent.
Equipped to serve, prepared to build,
Each calling shaped, each purpose filled.
The hand may teach, the eye may warn,
The feet may go where hope is born.
And all, when led by Christ the Head,
Grow up in truth, in love, and bread.


### Reflections from the Road

1. What does it mean for you to walk "worthy" of your calling?

2. How does Paul's model of leadership challenge the way churches often function today?

3. Where have you seen equipping ministry—preparing others to serve—done well?

4. What gifts has God given you; how can they be used in the body?

5. How would your church look different if every member lived out their ministry calling?

# 60

# How the Body Behaves

*Ephesians 4:17–5:21; Colossians 3:1–17*

Paul never writes theology for theology's sake. In nearly every letter, he follows exalted truths with practical commands—a seamless movement from **what we believe** to **how we live**.

To the Ephesians and the Colossians, this movement is striking. After unveiling the mystery of Christ, the unity of the Church, and the glory of grace, Paul says in effect: "Now walk like it."

He draws a line between **the old self** and **the new**, between life shaped by the world and life shaped by Christ. It is more than morality. It is **identity expressed through behavior**.

*"You must no longer walk as the Gentiles do..."* *"Put off the old self... be renewed... put on the new self..."* *"Set your minds on things above... put to death what is earthly in you..."*

Both letters follow this pattern:

- Ephesians 4:17–5:21 urges believers to walk in purity, love, light, and wisdom.

- Colossians 3:1–17 outlines virtues to put on and vices to put off.

Lying gives way to truth. Bitterness yields to forgiveness. Sexual immorality is replaced by holy love. Grumbling is swallowed up by gratitude. Selfishness bows to service.

*"Be imitators of God... walk in love..."* "Let the peace of Christ rule in your hearts..." *"Whatever you do, in word or deed, do everything in the name of the Lord Jesus..."*

Paul's vision is not merely ethical. It is **formational**. The Church is to be a **countercultural people**, shaped not by trends or appetites but by Christ Himself.

This is the "so what" of gospel doctrine.

In Romans 12:2, Paul had already said it:

*"Do not be conformed to this world, but be transformed by the renewing of your mind."*

The world will always try to press us into its mold—to define identity by achievement, sexuality, wealth, appearance, or tribe. But the Church stands apart. Not in arrogance, but in holiness. Not to withdraw, but to shine.

We were first called *Christians* not because we fit in, but because we stood out—**as Christ, like Christ.**

This is how the Body behaves: not as the world, but **as witnesses** to another Kingdom.

## "A People Set Apart"

No longer cast in worldly mold,
But shaped by hands of grace...
We walk in truth, we speak in peace,
We shine in every place.

Put off the dark, put on the light,
Put envy, rage, and pride away.
Let love be loud, let Christ be near,
Let mercy mark the narrow way.

## Reflections from the Road

1. Why does Paul move from theology to ethics in his letters?

2. What does it mean to *"put off the old self"* and *"put on the new"*?

3. How do the moral instructions in these letters reflect Christ's character?

4. Where do you feel the pressure to conform to the world's mold?

5. What would it look like for your church to be a people that truly *"shine as lights in the world"*?

# 61

# A Gospel of Welcome

## *Philemon*

The letter to Philemon is the shortest in Paul's collection—a private note about a runaway slave. But its implications reach far beyond household drama. In **just 25 verses**, Paul unfolds a powerful theology of **forgiveness, restoration, and gospel-shaped relationships**.

Onesimus had belonged to Philemon, a believer in Colossae. He ran. Somewhere along the way, he met Paul—perhaps in Rome, perhaps by divine appointment. Under Paul's influence, Onesimus became a follower of Christ.

Now Paul sends him back. Not as property. Not as a fugitive. But as a **brother**.

*"Perhaps the reason he was separated from you for a little while was that you might have him back forever—no longer as a slave, but better than a slave, as a dear brother"* (Philemon 15–16).

Paul makes no demand. He appeals. He doesn't command. He **persuades with love**, laying himself on the line:

*"If he owes you anything, charge it to me... I will repay."*

In these words, Paul steps into the place of Christ himself—interceding, reconciling, restoring.

Philemon is more than a personal letter. It is a case study in **how the gospel overturns status, reorders power, and redefines identity**. In Christ, slave and master are siblings. Property becomes personhood. Law bows to love.

It also gives us a glimpse of Paul the pastor. He doesn't treat theology as abstraction. He brings it into the real tensions of real lives—and lets grace lead the way.

What becomes of Onesimus after this? Tradition says he became a bishop in Ephesus. But Paul never tells us the outcome. Perhaps that's intentional. The letter leaves the reader with a question:

What will you do with this man, Philemon?
What will *you* do with the gospel?


## "A Place at the Table"

He came with chains, he left with grace,
Once out of place, now face to face.
No longer slave, no longer less—
Now clothed in Christ's own righteousness.

So welcome him as you would me,
For mercy makes the bound man free.
And if he wronged you, let it be—
I bear the debt. Charge it to me.


## Reflections from the Road

1. Why do you think Paul refused to command Philemon to forgive, but instead appealed in love?

2. How does the gospel challenge the social status systems of our world—then and now?

3. What do you think it meant for Onesimus to walk back into Philemon's household carrying this letter?

4. In what ways does Paul's attitude reflect Christ's role as mediator and reconciler?

5. Who in your life might need to be welcomed "no longer as a servant, but as a beloved brother"?

# 62

# Partners in the Gospel

## *Philippians 1:1–30*

Some churches Paul wrote to out of necessity. Corinth needed correction. Galatia needed rescuing. Thessalonica needed reassurance. But Philippi? Paul wrote them with **joy.**

This was the first church he planted in Europe. A Roman colony. A military town. A strategic place for the gospel to gain ground westward. And from the beginning, the Philippians were more than converts. They were *partners.*

Lydia, the seller of purple. The jailer, once trembling before an earthquake and an apostle. A church born out of power, prayer, and providence.

*"I thank my God upon every remembrance of you... always in every*

*prayer of mine for you all making my prayer with joy."*

Paul loved this church. And more than love, he **trusted** them. They had supported him again and again—from Thessalonica to Corinth, from prison cells to mission fields. When others forgot, the Philippians remembered.

*"From the first day until now... you are all partakers with me of grace, both in my imprisonment and in the defense and confirmation of the gospel."*

Without them, who knows? Perhaps two journeys, not three. Perhaps eight letters, not thirteen. The Philippians didn't preach from pulpits, but they **funded the movement**.

And Paul felt that deeply.

His prayer for them (vv. 9–11) is among the most beautiful in Scripture: abounding love, growing knowledge, discernment, sincerity, fruitfulness. He wanted their spiritual lives to be as rich as their generosity.

But even this warm letter carries a sober note.

*"Let your manner of life be worthy of the gospel..."* *"It has been granted to you... to believe in Him and also to suffer for His sake."*

Paul reminds them—and us—that suffering isn't a failure of faith. It's part of the package. Those who walk in Christ will also walk **in His conflict**.

Enemies of Paul will be enemies of the Philippians. And if Christ is Lord, Caesar is not. The gospel is subversive. Joyful, yes. But dangerous. Glorious, yes. But costly.

So Paul urges them:

- **Stand firm.**
- **Strive together.**
- **Live like citizens of another Kingdom.**

They were not spectators. They were soldiers. Saints. Partners in the gospel.

## "The First to Stand With Me"

A woman by the river's grace,
A jailer rescued, fear erased.
Together formed a gospel flame,
That bore the weight of Jesus' name.

When others failed to understand,
You stood with me, a faithful band.
So now I write with joy and pride,
For saints who never left my side.

## Reflections from the Road

1. How does Philippi's role as the first European church affect how we read this letter?

2. Why do you think Paul felt such affection for the Philippians?

3. What does it mean to be a *"partner in the gospel"*?

4. How do generosity and suffering both shape the life of the Church?

5. Where do you see yourself in the Philippians' story—as a supporter, a sufferer, a joyful partner?

# 63

# We Sang the Word

## *Philippians 2:5–11*

The flickering lamplight casts long shadows across the room.
In a humble home somewhere in Philippi, a gathering of believers
lifts their voices in unison. No stage. No spotlight. Just hearts and
harmonies shaped by truth. They do not merely sing about Christ.
They sing Christ Himself.

*"Who, though He was in the form of God, did not count equality
with God a thing to be grasped..."*

These words were not written as a doctrinal lecture. They were sung.
A hymn.

The early church embedded theology in its worship. They sang the
Word:

- To remember who Jesus is.

- To model the humility of Christ.

- To let doctrine become devotion.

In these verses, Paul quotes a song already known to the church. Its
rhythm carried revelation. Its lines carved identity.

*"He emptied Himself... taking the form of a servant... He humbled
Himself..."*

The Greek verb *ekenōsen* does not mean Christ ceased to be divine.
He laid aside—not His deity—but the privileges, prerogatives, and
visible majesty of His divine rank. As J.B. Lightfoot put it, "He di-
vested Himself of the insignia of majesty." He added to Himself the

nature of a slave while retaining the nature of God.

And crucially, the Greek word for "*Himself*" (*heauton*) is reflexive—underscoring that the emptying and humbling were self-initiated. The Son was not stripped of His glory by another. He laid it aside willingly.

As J.B. Phillips beautifully paraphrased,

"*He, who had always been God by nature, did not cling to His prerogatives as God's equal, but stripped Himself of all privilege...*"

Jesus didn't cling to His privileges. He chose a cross over a crown. His descent was voluntary. He humbled Himself.

This hymn wasn't just high theology. It was also pastoral correction. Paul offered it to call the Philippians away from rivalry and pride, into unity and humility:
"*Let each of you look not only to his own interests, but also to the interests of others. Have this mind among yourselves...*"

Their worship was meant to shape their walk.

This, perhaps, is what the modern church has lost. We have moved from Christ-centered hymns of incarnation and glory to songs filled with "me" and "my." We have exchanged mystery for mood, substance for style.

But the early church knew: we don't just worship what we believe; we begin to believe what we sing.

The Word was sung before it was systematized.
It formed hearts before it framed seminaries.

We sang the Word, not just about it—
And knelt beneath its flame-lit weight.

### "Kenosis"

He laid aside His rightful throne,
Clothed glory in a servant's form;
Not less divine, but veiled and low,
To walk where weary sinners go.
He did not cling, He did not grasp,
But bent beneath obedience' task.
And rising, crowned with heaven's acclaim,
We sing the worth of Jesus' name.


### Reflections from the Road

1. What does Philippians 2:5–11 reveal about the nature and character of Christ?

2. How does the image of Jesus laying aside His privileges reshape your understanding of leadership and service?

3. What does it mean to say, "We begin to believe what we sing"?

4. How might we reclaim worship that forms us theologically, not just emotionally?

5. In what ways can humility, as modeled by Jesus, transform your relationships within the Body of Christ?

# 64

# Pressing Toward the Prize

## *Philippians 3:1–21*

Paul knew what it meant to be a spiritual success by human stand-ards. A Hebrew of Hebrews. A Pharisee. Blameless under the Law. He had climbed the religious ladder—and then he met Jesus.

And everything changed.

*"Whatever gain I had, I counted as loss for the sake of Christ... I count them as rubbish, in order that I may gain Christ."*

This was no mild reordering of priorities. It was a radical renuncia-tion. The pearl of great price had been found. The treasure buried in the field uncovered. And Paul was willing to part with every creden-tial, title, and boast to gain something greater: **Christ Himself.**

Chapter 3 begins with a warning: beware of those who add to grace. The old enemies of Paul's gospel—the Jesus-plus teachers—were still at work. Their message was subtle: faith in Jesus is good, but not enough. Circumcision, Law-keeping, ritual purity—these were being pushed as supplements to salvation.

Paul would have none of it. His story was the refutation.

*"Not having a righteousness of my own that comes from the law, but that which comes through faith in Christ..."*

This is the gospel he fought for in Galatians. This is the righteous-ness he exalted in Romans. Here in Philippians, he personalizes it.

But Paul doesn't stop with justification. He presses forward into sanctification:

*"Not that I have already obtained it... but I press on to make it my own, because Christ Jesus has made me His own."*

Paul runs like a man who knows the finish line is worth it.

He forgets what is behind—whether success or shame. And like the writer of Hebrews, he fixes his eyes on Jesus (Heb. 12:1-2).

*"This one thing I do... I press on toward the goal for the prize of the upward call of God in Christ Jesus."*

He invites the mature to follow his example. And not just his. Any who walk this way. Because the world is full of voices that mock this race, that live for appetite and glory in shame.

*"Their end is destruction... But our citizenship is in heaven."*

This world is not our home. We live by a different hope. We await a Savior who will transform our lowly bodies to be like His glorious one.

This is no passive waiting. This is **active pursuit**.

*We strain ahead, not to earn Christ, but because we have been caught by Him.*


### "The Upward Call"

I ran with robes and titles proud,
Till Love unrobed me in the crowd.
Now clothed in grace, I run anew,
With eyes on Christ, the prize in view.

Forget the past—the loss, the gain,
The chains of guilt, the crowns of fame.
For all of it is dust and dim,
Compared to knowing more of Him.

**Reflections from the Road**

What does Paul's willingness to count all things as loss teach us about true spiritual priorities?

How does Philippians 3 reinforce the gospel of grace Paul proclaimed in Galatians and Romans?

Why is it important to forget "what lies behind" in our spiritual walk?

Who are the examples of faithful pursuit in your life? Who is following your example?

How does the promise of transformation in verses 20–21 anchor our present pursuit of Christ?

# 65

# The Secret of Contentment

## *Philippians 4:4–19*

Of all the places to write about contentment, **prison** seems the least likely. Yet it is from confinement—chained, watched, dependent on others—that Paul pens some of his most liberating words:

*"I have learned, in whatever state I am, to be content."*

Not resigned. Not passive. **Content.**

This kind of peace doesn't come naturally. It is learned. It is practiced. And Paul gives us the path:

## 1. The Power of Prayer (Philippians 4:4–7)

*"Do not be anxious about anything, but in everything, by prayer and supplication with thanksgiving, let your requests be made known to God..."*

Pray about everything. Worry about nothing. Be thankful for anything. And the peace of God will *guard* your heart like a fortress. The Greek word here paints the image of a garrison—a divine keep around your thoughts.

## 2. The Power of Positive Thinking (Philippians 4:8–9)

*"Whatever is true, noble, right, pure, lovely, admirable... think about these things."*

Paul understood: the mind is a battlefield. What we feed it shapes what we feel. Discipline your thoughts, and you direct your soul. This is not empty optimism—it is **Christ-anchored attentiveness** to what builds faith.

## 3. The Power of a Person (Philippians 4:10–13)

*"I have learned the secret... I can do all things through Christ who strengthens me."*

Paul wasn't denying pain or pretending hardship didn't exist. He was testifying: **Christ is enough.**

This isn't a magic verse for athletes or impossible feats. It's not about lifting weights or leaping hurdles. It's about **enduring with grace, trusting in lack, overflowing in love.**

The Philippians had renewed their support of Paul's ministry. He could almost see them—Lydia, the wealthy merchant; the jailer who once feared for his life; the young girl once chained by a demon, now free in Christ—all passing the hat to help their beloved mentor.

And Paul thanked them. Not out of desperation, but appreciation:

*"Not that I seek the gift, but I seek the fruit that increases to your credit..."*

Their gift was more than material support. It was worship. A sweet-smelling sacrifice.

And Paul gave them a promise in return:

*"My God will supply all your needs according to His riches in glory in Christ Jesus."*

Here is a life worth imitating:

- **Gratitude without greed.**

- **Strength without striving.**

- **Contentment without complacency.**

Wherever you are, live here.

### "Have Learned"

Not from plenty, not from pain,
But walking through the loss and gain—
I learned to lean, to yield, to rest,
To trust that God would choose the best.

In prayers I whispered, tears I shed,
He brought me peace, and daily bread.
No golden path, no velvet throne,
Just Christ—and Christ alone.

### Reflections from the Road

1. How does Paul's view of contentment challenge modern definitions of success?

2. What role does prayer play in shaping your emotional and spiritual peace?

3. Why is it important to be mindful of the thoughts we dwell on, according to Paul?

4. What does Philippians 4:13 mean in its actual context?

5. Have you ever experienced the kind of mutual support that Paul and the Philippians shared? How did it affect your faith?

# Interlude: The Last Letters

## *1 Timothy, Titus, 2 Timothy*

Paul was nearing the end.

He had traveled thousands of miles, planted churches from Antioch to Corinth, debated in synagogues, preached on hillsides, and written letters that would outlast empires. But now, with the days growing shorter, Paul wasn't looking for one more journey. He was looking for **a legacy**.

The final three letters that bear his name—**1 Timothy**, **Titus**, and **2 Timothy**—are not sweeping theological treatises like Romans, or poetic hymns like Philippians. They are letters from an older man to two younger ones. From a spiritual father to his sons in the faith. These are **the Pastorals**.

They are Paul's final investment in the next generation.

## 1 Timothy & Titus: Sons with a Charge

Paul had entrusted Timothy to shepherd the church in **Ephesus**, the jewel of Asia. A rich, cosmopolitan city, home to the Temple of Artemis and a thriving church. But Ephesus was also a place of distraction, danger, and doctrinal drift. Paul urged Timothy to stand firm, to "*stir up the gift*" within him, and to **teach sound doctrine**.

Meanwhile, Titus had been sent to **Crete**. Tougher terrain. Rougher people. A messier church. Titus was older, perhaps more seasoned, and Paul gave him a high-stakes assignment: "*Set in order what remains... and appoint elders in every city.*"

Both letters carry shared themes:

- **Sound doctrine** (used repeatedly)

- **Leadership development**

- **Moral example**

- **Guarding the faith from false teachers**

Paul saw doctrine not as dusty theory but as **life-giving truth**. He told Timothy and Titus to *teach what accords with sound doctrine*, to *guard the deposit*, to *rightly handle the word of truth*.

He gave them clear instruction for building a healthy, durable church:

- **Bishops/elders/pastors** who are grounded, faithful, respected

- **Deacons** who serve with integrity, not driven by ego or greed

Paul's leadership model was never a one-man show. He built **teams**, **structures**, and **systems** that could outlive him. And he expected Timothy and Titus to do the same.

"*Entrust what you have learned to faithful men who will be able to teach others also...*" (2 Tim. 2:2)

This is not institutionalism. It's discipleship with a long view.


## 2 Timothy: The Farewell

Then comes 2 Timothy.

Written from a Roman prison, this letter hums with finality. The tone has shifted. Paul knows: "*The time of my departure is at hand.*"

And what matters most at the end?

- **Faithful friends**: *Bring John Mark.*

- **Simple comforts**: *Bring my cloak.*

- **Mental firewood**: *Bring my books.*

- **Eternal truths**: *Especially the parchments.*

Paul urges Timothy to "*preach the word*", to "*endure hardship*", to "*do the work of an evangelist*". He reflects on a life poured out like a drink offering. And he passes the torch.

These letters are Paul's final training sessions, final challenge, and final goodbye.


## Legacy

He speaks to **leadership**. He speaks to **truth**. He speaks to **faithfulness**.

And he asks one simple thing: *Don't let it die with me.*

Build something that will last. Entrust it to others. Preach what is true. Live what is right.

That's Paul's legacy. And ours to carry.

# 66

# Blueprints for the Church

## *1 Timothy 3:1–13; Titus 1:5–9*

The gospel always creates community. But to grow strong, that community must be *ordered*. Paul knew that churches weren't just gatherings of people but living, breathing expressions of the Body of Christ. And like everybody, they needed *structure*. Not rigid control. Not hierarchy. But **form that could carry function**.

As Paul neared the end of his ministry, he passed the baton to his trusted sons—Timothy and Titus—and gave them *blueprints*. Not for buildings, but for **spiritual leadership** that could outlast his own presence.

To **Titus**, sent to untamed Crete, Paul wrote: "*Set in order what remains and appoint elders in every town.*" Leadership wasn't optional. It was essential. Healthy churches don't just happen.

To **Timothy**, overseeing the complex work at Ephesus, Paul laid out qualifications for two types of leaders: **elders (also called bishops or pastors)** and **deacons**. The focus wasn't on title, but on **character**:

- Above reproach

- Faithful in relationships

- Self-controlled, hospitable, not quarrelsome

- Not greedy, but generous

- Able to teach (for elders), and spiritually mature (for all)

What mattered most wasn't giftedness but **godliness**.

In both letters, Paul emphasized that these leaders must *first be tested* and must *manage their households well*. Why? Because the Church isn't a corporation—it's a **spiritual family**. Leaders must lead as spiritual fathers, not CEOs.

In my own sense of ministry calling: leaders are to be equippers of the saints for their work of ministry so that the Body will be built up.

Leadership is never about platform—it's about **preparation**. Paul knew that churches grow strong when leaders multiply, when service is shared, and when the focus stays on **Christ, not charisma**.

This is why Paul was so clear. If the Church is to last, it must be:

- Built on **shared responsibility**, not spiritual celebrity

- Led by **servants**, not performers

Structured with **biblical clarity**, not personal ambition
Whether a small-town congregation or a city church, these blueprints remain. Every faithful church still draws from this pattern today.


## "Foundation Lines"

Not towers high nor marble walls,
Not gilded thrones or hallowed halls,
But hearts made clean and hands held fast,
By truth that shines and love that lasts.
A shepherd's strength, a servant's way,
A steady voice that will not sway,
These are the stones that shape the frame,
And hold aloft the Savior's name.

1. What qualities do you value most in spiritual leaders? How do these align with Paul's blueprints?

2. Why does Paul prioritize character over skill in church leadership?

3. How can your church identify and support those who may be called to serve as elders or deacons?

4. What might shared leadership look like in your context?

5. Are there ways you can personally support or encourage those who carry the weight of church leadership?

# 67

# Guard the Deposit

## *1 Timothy 1:3–7; 4:1–16; Titus 2:1*

Doctrine isn't just for dusty classrooms. It's the difference between a church that stands and a church that drifts.

Paul was urgent. Timothy had been left in Ephesus, not for convenience, but for a charge: *"stay there...so that you may command certain people not to teach false doctrines."* (1 Tim. 1:3)

Truth matters. Not as trivia, but as **soul-anchoring reality**. The early church didn't flourish because it had good vibes and clever slogans. It flourished because it was *rooted* in truth that transformed.

But false teaching was already on the rise—speculations, myths, distractions that pulled believers away from "*a pure heart and a good conscience and a sincere faith*" (1:5). Paul called it out as early as Galatians and now, in his final season, he's still fighting the same war.

In 1 Timothy 4, Paul laid it out plainly: "*The Spirit clearly says that in later times some will abandon the faith...*"

- They will follow deceptive spirits.

- They will forbid what God has permitted.

- They will twist truth into control.

And so Paul told Timothy: "*Until I come, devote yourself to the public reading of Scripture, to preaching and to teaching... Watch your life and doctrine closely. Persevere in them, because if you do, you will save both yourself and your hearers.*" (4:13, 16)

To Titus, he gave the same instruction in compressed form: "*Teach what accords with sound doctrine.*" (Titus 2:1)

This wasn't about winning debates. It was about **protecting souls**.

Truth doesn't just *inform* the church—it **forms** the church. What we believe shapes how we live. And if what we believe is shallow, sensational, or skewed, the church becomes unstable, vulnerable, and ineffective.

We are still called to guard the deposit. Not with arrogance. Not with fear. But with **fidelity**. Because healthy churches are not built on trends, speculations, or spiritual fads. They are built on truth that endures.

### "Guard the Flame"

Not every wind is Spirit-breathed,
Not every word is true,
Not every voice that claims the light

219

Is bringing light to you.
But anchored deep in sacred page,
And formed in holy flame,
The truth of God still lights the path
For those who guard the Name.

## Reflections from the Road

1. What does it mean to "*guard the deposit*" of faith in your own life and church?

2. How can sound doctrine be taught in ways that build up rather than divide?

3. Are there any "trends or speculations" that are distracting from the gospel in your context?

4. How are you engaging with Scripture regularly, both privately and publicly?

5. What role does doctrine play in the spiritual health of your family or congregation?

# 68

# The Example You Set

## *1 Timothy 4:12; Titus 2:7–8*

Before Paul gave Timothy a preaching plan, he gave him a personal one:

*"Let no one look down on you because you are young, but set an example for the believers in speech, in conduct, in love, in faith, and in purity."* (1 Tim. 4:12)

This wasn't a pep talk. It was a strategy. In a world full of opinions, Paul reminded Timothy: **you are the message.**

People may question your theology. They may resist your teaching. But they cannot ignore a life well-lived.

Paul wasn't telling Timothy to be perfect—he was telling him to be *consistent*. The young leader would win respect not through credentials, but by character:

- **Speech** that is honest and grace-filled

- **Conduct** that mirrors Christ

- **Love** that puts others first

- **Faith** that trusts God openly

- **Purity** that refuses to compromise

To Titus, Paul wrote the same blueprint:

*"Show yourself in all respects to be a model of good works, and in your teaching show integrity, dignity, and sound speech that cannot be condemned..."* (Titus 2:7–8)

The principle is clear: **People follow your life before they follow your teaching.**

In today's church culture—with platforms and podcasts, branding and charisma—this reminder is needed more than ever.

Spiritual leadership isn't performance. It's **presence**. The kind of presence that says: *"Imitate me as I imitate Christ."*

Whether you're leading a congregation, a small group, or your family—your life is your loudest sermon.

## "Your Life Is the Lesson"

You may not preach from pulpit high,
Or hold a scholar's pen,
But in your words and in your walk,
You lead the hearts of men.
A tone that calms, a hand that lifts,
A heart that points above—
These speak with power, more than creeds,
When shaped by faith and love.

## Reflections from the Road

1. In what ways are you already "setting an example" for those around you?

2. Which area (speech, conduct, love, faith, purity) is God currently refining in you?

3. How can church leaders better model faithfulness for those they serve?

4. Who has been a living example of Christ to you? What did you notice most?

5. What small daily choices can you make that leave a lasting spiritual impression?

# 69

# A Culture of Discipleship

## *Titus 2:1–8; 1 Timothy 5*

Churches don't grow by programs alone. They grow when *people pour into people.*

Paul saw this clearly. Discipleship was not a ministry silo or a special class. It was the very fabric of Christian life—woven into conversations, relationships, and daily rhythms. This is why he gave Titus such a practical vision:

*"Teach what is appropriate to sound doctrine... Older men are to be sober-minded... Older women likewise... so that they may encourage the young women... Likewise urge the young men... In everything show yourself to be an example..."* (Titus 2:1–8)

Paul cast a **multi-generational vision**: the entire community of faith shaping one another, each generation lifting the next.

This is discipleship at its best:

- Rooted in **relationship**

- Anchored in **truth**

- Focused on **life change**

In 1 Timothy 5, Paul gave guidance on how the church should treat older and younger believers, widows and families—not as categories of concern, but as **circles of care**. Within these instructions, we hear a powerful implication: *The church is a family, and every generation has a part to play in forming the next.*

This is sustainable ministry. Not dependent on one pastor. Not built around a few leaders. But a **culture of spiritual parenting** where maturity means multiplication.

Paul modeled this himself:

*"The things you have heard from me... entrust to faithful men who will be able to teach others also."* (2 Tim. 2:2)

Four generations of disciples in one sentence.

The Church grows stronger when everyone is investing in someone else. Not as a task. But as a lifestyle.

## "Tell the Next"

One voice speaks truth, another hears,
Then carries light through passing years.
A hand to guide, a heart to share,
A love that listens, lifts, and dares.
The Church is not a stage or show,
But seed and root and branch that grow.
So tell the next, and tell again,
Until the faith is born in them.

## Reflections from the Road

1. Who has poured into your life spiritually? How did they shape your faith?

2. Are you currently investing in someone else's spiritual journey?

3. What barriers keep churches from embracing intergenerational discipleship?

4. How can your church foster a culture where every member is both a learner and a mentor?

5. What simple, intentional step could you take this week to disciple or encourage someone else?

# 70

# Equippers, Not Entertainers

*Ephesians 4:11–16; Titus 1:5–9; 1 Timothy 3:1–7;*

*Colossians 1:28*

In a time when churches look to pastors as CEOs, celebrities, or spiritual stand-up comedians, the apostolic vision remains stubbornly—and beautifully—different.

Paul had no use for stagecraft. What he needed—and what the churches needed—were equippers.

That's what Timothy and Titus were tasked with building: not just congregations, but leadership. Paul reminded both men that the church would never rise above its maturity unless its leaders first understood their own calling. Not to dominate. Not to dazzle. But to develop—to equip the saints for the work of ministry.

We find the qualifications of these key leaders of a congregation in the instructions to both Timothy (1 Timothy 3:1-7) and Titus (Titus 1:5-11). These men were not instructed in lighting and PR—they were instructed in the doctrines of the faith and were urged to teach, to exhort (encourage), and to convince.

The Greek word *katartizo*, translated "equip," paints a vivid picture of what these leaders of the flock were to do. It means to mend a net, to supply a soldier, to furnish a craftsman with tools. It is slow work. Pastoral work. And it's the only kind of leadership that builds a church strong enough to last.

Paul's directive was clear: raise up leaders of godly character who could model truth and teach sound doctrine. Not prima donnas. Not crowd-pleasers. But shepherds. Teachers. Examples.

To the Ephesians, Paul described the purpose of this kind of leadership:

*"...until we all attain to the unity of the faith and of the knowledge of the Son of God, to a mature man... no longer children, tossed to and fro... but speaking the truth in love, we are to grow up in all aspects into Him who is the head..."* (Eph. 4:13–15)

Healthy churches don't grow by accident. They grow when leaders equip believers, when believers do the work of ministry, and when all are built up together in love.

To this end, Paul told the Colossians:

*"We proclaim Him, admonishing and teaching everyone with all wisdom, so that we may present everyone complete in Christ."* (Col. 1:28)

That's the job. Not filling seats. Not drawing fans. Presenting people *complete in Christ.*

It's time to recover the vision. Pastors as equippers. Churches as training grounds. Every believer—trained, mobilized, and growing.

Not performers.
*Equippers.*


### "Tools in Hand"

Not to impress, but to prepare,
Not to perform, but to repair—
A net once torn, now stretched and mended,
A sword once dulled, now burnished, tended.
The goal is not applause, but growth,
A faith alive, a sacred oath—
To train, to send, to shape, to teach,
That all might grasp what few can preach.

**Reflections from the Road**

1. How does Paul's vision for church leadership differ from what we often see today?

2. What does *equipping the saints* look like in your context?

3. What are the dangers of replacing discipleship with entertainment or performance?

4. How does Colossians 1:28 challenge or inspire your own sense of calling?

5. Who has equipped you in your own journey? And who are you equipping now?

# The Farewell: 2 Timothy

# 71

## Dispatch from the Front

### *2 Timothy 1:6–14*

This was no armchair reflection. Paul wrote 2 Timothy from a cold Roman cell, chained as a criminal, nearing the end of his race. But his tone wasn't resignation—it was **resolve**. This was a dispatch from the front lines of faith.

To Timothy, his young protégé who wrestled with fear and timidity, Paul sent a rallying cry:

*"Fan into flame the gift of God... For God gave us not a spirit of fear but of power and love and self-control."* (2 Tim. 1:6–7)

Timothy didn't need a new calling. He needed to *rekindle* the fire.

Paul knew the cost of ministry. He bore it in his scars. But he also knew its **power**. And he charged Timothy—and through him, *all who would lead*—to rise with:

**Boldness** in the face of opposition

**Faithfulness** in guarding the gospel

**Clarity** about who he served

*"Do not be ashamed of the testimony about our Lord, nor of me his prisoner, but share in suffering for the gospel by the power of God."* (1:8)

This wasn't just about endurance. It was about **entrustment**:

*"What you heard from me, keep as the pattern of sound teaching, with faith and love in Christ Jesus. Guard the good deposit..."* (1:13 –14)

The gospel had been placed in Timothy's hands like a flame passed in darkness. And Paul's message was clear:

**Don't let it go out.**

Leadership in the church has never been about comfort. It's about **courage**. It's about holding fast to what is true and passing it on with conviction. Even in chains, Paul wrote like a free man. And his charge echoes still: guard the gospel, stir the gift, suffer well, stand strong.

This is frontline faith.

## "Fan the Flame"

The coals grow dim, the wind is cold,
The world says, "Quiet now, grow old."
But grace still burns, and truth still glows,

And Spirit fire within still grows.
So stir it up, though night be near,
Let boldness rise, let go of fear.
For gospel light is not a game—
Guard the trust, and fan the flame.

### Reflections from the Road

1. What fears or pressures tempt you to shrink back in your calling?

2. How do you "fan into flame" the gift God has given you?

3. What does it mean to not be ashamed of the gospel in today's culture?

4. Who has entrusted truth to you? How are you passing it on?

5. In what ways can your suffering or difficulty become a testimony to others?

# 72

# The Word and the Work

## *2 Timothy 3:14–4:5*

The church doesn't run on personality, trend, or hype. It runs on **truth**.

Paul, facing the final stretch of his life, left Timothy a tool that would outlast empires and ideologies:

*"All Scripture is God-breathed and is useful for teaching, rebuking, correcting and training in righteousness, so that the servant of God*

*may be thoroughly equipped for every good work."* (2 Tim. 3:16–17)

The Word is the tool. The Word is the fuel. The Word is the map.

Paul didn't hand Timothy a plan for church growth or a manifesto for relevance. He handed him **the Scriptures**:

- Breathed by God

- Useful for daily life

- Sufficient to equip God's people


Then came the charge:

*"Preach the Word; be ready in season and out of season; reprove, rebuke, and exhort, with complete patience and teaching."* (4:2)

Paul saw what was coming. He warned of a time when people would turn from truth to myth, from sound teaching to pleasing distractions. That time isn't coming—*it's here.*

In the noise of our age, the Word is still **the clear note**. In the confusion, it is **the anchor**. In the assignment, it is **the equipping**.

Scripture isn't a book of reference. It is our **source of readiness**. And Paul made it personal: *"As for you..."* (3:14, 4:5)

Hold fast. Lean in. Finish your work with the only thing powerful enough to sustain it.

Servants of God are made ready, not by title or talent, but by truth.


### "The Tool and the Flame"

A sacred breath on every page,
A light that burns through every age,
A sword to cut, a balm to heal,
A word to shape the heart of steel.

When winds of change and shadows play,
It marks the path, it shows the way.
So hold it fast, both night and day—
The Word, the work, the narrow way.

**Reflections from the Road**

1. How has Scripture shaped your understanding of your calling or ministry?

2. What makes the Bible different from all other books?

3. In what ways are you tempted to rely on things other than Scripture to do God's work?

4. Are you *"ready in season and out"* to share truth, rebuke, encourage?

5. How can you help others develop confidence in the sufficiency of God's Word?

# 73

# Finished, But Not Done

## *2 Timothy 4:6–22*

The light in the cell was dim, the chill creeping through Roman stones, winter pressing in. The days of travel and teaching, of synagogue debates and shipwrecks, were now memories etched into the body of a man who had spent his life for Christ.

But Paul was not afraid.

*"For I am already being poured out as a drink offering, and the time of my departure has come."* (2 Tim. 4:6)

He had been poured out. Every last drop of passion, wisdom, and witness offered in service to the One who had met him on the Damascus Road. The time of his departure was at hand—not a collapse, not a failure, but a departure. Like a ship loosed from its moorings, heading home.

*"I have fought the good fight, I have finished the race, I have kept the faith."* (4:7)

Yes. The battles had been fierce—external and internal. Persecutions, prisons, betrayals, sleepless nights, and daily concern for the churches. He had fought to protect the gospel from distortion, to guard the faith from fear, to build the Body with his own battered hands.

The race marked out for him had taken him farther than he imagined. From Tarsus to Jerusalem, from Antioch to Athens, from the halls of power to the margins of empire. He had not drifted from the path. He had run with endurance.

To the end. Through suffering and success, through praise and stoning, through loneliness and joy. He had guarded the treasure entrusted to him. And now, with hands open and heart full, he prepared to return it to the King.

*"Henceforth there is laid up for me the crown of righteousness... and not only to me but also to all who have loved His appearing."* (4:8)

A crown. Not the fading laurels of Rome, but the crown of righteousness. A reward not earned, but bestowed by the Righteous Judge—Jesus, his Lord.

This was no farewell in despair. It was a victory speech. A final benediction. A whisper into the dark: *The King is coming.*

And the Kingdom... has no end.

Even in these last verses, the human touches stir us:

- *"Bring the cloak"* – the body still felt the cold.

- *"Bring the scrolls, especially the parchments"* – the mind still thirsted for truth.

- *"Bring John Mark, for he is useful to me"* – the heart still longed for restored friendship.

Faithful to the end, Paul closed his final letter with hope, not regret. And in doing so, he handed the torch to us.

## "A Life Poured Out"

The road was long, the race well run,
The fight endured, the course was done.
With empty hands and steady breath,
He smiled into the face of death.
Not with fear, but eyes on grace,
He saw beyond the prison place,
To crowns not forged by earthly hands,
To home, and light, and promised lands.
So pass it on, this sacred fire,
This holy call, this heart's desire.
Finish well, and you shall see
The King in all His majesty.

## Reflections from the Road

1. What does it mean to *"fight the good fight"* in your own season of life?

2. Are you running the race marked out for you, or someone else's?

3. How can you keep the faith with both passion and perseverance?

4. Who do you need to restore, encourage, or bring along in these final laps?

5. What legacy of faith are you building to pass on to others?

## Author's Note:

We read Paul's last words to Timothy and we think these are his last. But they are not in certain senses. Throughout Paul's letters, we find him praying for individuals and for churches he planted and nurtured. In a sense, Paul prayed not just for them—but for us as well. Prayers do not have an expiration date stamped on them. Paul's prayers lodged in the heart of our heavenly Father and are still being honored for His people.

Paul wrote letters to individuals and to followers of Jesus in cities in Asia and Europe. But like his prayers, his letters were not just to the recipients. Peter noted that the writings of Paul were already at the early stage of the church considered Scripture (2 Peter 3:14-18). Those letters became a major portion of the New Testament in our Bible. Why? Because we as the early church feel the breath of God in them.

# 74

# That You May Know and Be Filled

## *Ephesians 1:16–23; 3:14–21*

Paul didn't just preach to the churches he founded. He prayed for them—fervently, specifically, and expansively. His letters to the Ephesians preserve two of the most profound prayers in the New Testament, windows into what Paul believed every believer truly needed.

In the first, Paul prayed that the eyes of their hearts would be enlightened—to grasp the hope of God's calling, the riches of His inheritance, and the incomparable greatness of His power. This was not a prayer for ease or security, but for vision and boldness. He wanted them to know who they were and what God had done.

In the second, Paul knelt and prayed again—for strength in the inner being, for rootedness in love, and for a grasp of the immeasurable dimensions of Christ's love. He asked that they be filled *"to all the fullness of God."*

Paul's intercession was not casual. It was architectural. He prayed the church into strength, maturity, and awe.

### "That Christ May Dwell"
I do not ask for wealth or ease,
For status, strength, or fleeting peace.
But this I ask from bended knee—
That Christ may dwell and live in thee.
That rooted deep in love you grow,
And heights of mercy come to know.

That power—not of man but God—
May walk with you where saints have trod.
To grasp how wide, how long, how high,
The love that placed His throne nearby.
And having tasted grace so vast,
Be filled with fullness unsurpassed.
So I, though bound, still lift my voice,
To mark your hearts with Spirit's choice.
For you are His, and I remain—
A servant praying in His name.


## Reflections from the Road

1. When you pray for others, what do you typically ask God to do? How do Paul's prayers challenge or reshape your focus?

2. What does it mean to be "strengthened in your inner being"? How is that different from outward strength?

3. Take a moment to reflect on the dimensions of Christ's love—its breadth, length, height, and depth. Which aspect feels closest to your current journey?

4. What would it look like to be *filled to the measure of all the fullness of God*? Is that a concept of capacity, surrender, or both?

5. Try writing your own prayer for someone you care about, inspired by the themes in Ephesians 1 and 3.

# 75

# Breath of God

## *2 Peter 3:14–18*

Peter's last words to the early church did not focus on his own ministry—but on Paul's.

In the closing verses of his second letter, Peter urged believers to live in peace and holiness, to be vigilant against distortion, and to grow in grace. But most striking of all, he referred to Paul's writings—and called them Scripture. Even as Paul's life and mission drew to a close, the Holy Spirit was breathing something eternal through his pen.

Peter acknowledged that Paul's letters were sometimes hard to understand. He knew that unstable people would twist them. But he also recognized their divine origin. What Paul wrote was not just pastoral counsel or missionary strategy—it was sacred. Inspired. Binding. Alive.

Paul's letters, like his prayers, were not sealed in the first century. They still speak. They still cut and comfort, teach and warn, build and fill. The breath of God is still in them.


**"Breath of God"**
These were no idle scribbled notes,
No worn debates or passing quotes—
But words that burned through chains and stone,
That spoke with fire not their own.
Peter saw what others missed:
The Spirit traced through Paul's clenched fist.
Each scroll, each ink-lined page he bore,

Still echoes now—and evermore.
Hard to grasp? At times, yes.
But truth is weighty nonetheless.
And those who twist will find their shame
Before the One from whom it came.
But for the faithful, these endure—
A lamp to light, a seal secure.
The breath of God in mortal phrase,
Still calling out in latter days.


## Reflections from the Road

1. Why do you think Peter referred to Paul's letters as "Scripture"? What does that say about how early the church recognized their authority?

2. How do you respond to Peter's caution that Paul's writings could be "distorted"? Have you ever seen that happen?

3. What's the difference between *reading* Paul's letters and *receiving* them as the living word of God?

4. Which letter of Paul has spoken most deeply to you—and why?

5. How might your view of the Bible change if you remembered that the breath of God still rests upon its words?

# Epilogue

## *The Story Isn't Over*

Paul's journey ended in a Roman cell. But his mission didn't.

From Jerusalem to Rome, from synagogue to street corner, from parchment to pulpit, the flame that burned in him has never been extinguished. His words still echo in every generation that opens the Scriptures, lifts its eyes, and hears the call: *Follow me, as I follow Christ.*

He was not perfect. He bore the weight of regret and the scars of persecution. He knew what it was to be misunderstood, maligned, even abandoned. But he also knew this:

*"I am not ashamed of the gospel... it is the power of God for salvation."*
*"Christ lives in me."*
*"I press on."*
*"I have fought the good fight."*

Paul never saw ministry as performance. He saw it as a pouring out.

Every sermon, every journey, every letter—an offering. Every prison, every confrontation, every hardship—an act of faith. His ministry was not built on charisma but conviction. Not on cleverness, but cross-bearing. Not on brilliance, but bold obedience.

And now, the torch he carried is in your hands.

The churches he planted—are you helping plant more?
The truths he defended—are you guarding them with love and courage?
The people he discipled—are you raising your own?
The gospel he suffered for—does it still move you to tears, to action, to joy?

The Christian life is not inherited. It's embraced.
The Church doesn't grow by default. It grows by discipleship.
Paul didn't just write theology. He lived it. So must we.

So now, beloved reader—
Whether you are old or young, weary or just beginning,
Whether you lead a church, a classroom, or your family,
Whether you've failed or flourished,
There is still road ahead.

Take up the gospel.
Step into the story.
Finish your course.
Keep the faith.

The world doesn't need more influencers. It needs more Pauls.
And the Spirit of God still says, "*Set apart for me... the ones I will send.*"


The profiles from Paul end here.

But your chapter may just be beginning.

# Get the Companion:

## *Beyond Expectations*
## The Kingdom No One Expected

**What kind of Kingdom begins with a cross?**

Jesus came preaching the Kingdom of God—but not the one anyone expected.

*Beyond Expectations: The Kingdom No One Expected* invites you into 55 vivid vignettes—each a devotional window into the life of Jesus and the surprising nature of His reign. From the wedding at Cana to the cry from the cross, these reflections trace the arc of a Kingdom not built on conquest, but on compassion; not rooted in might, but in mercy.

Blending pastoral warmth, poetic insight, and biblical depth, this is **devotional theology**—Scripture brought to life in ways both reverent and real.

Whether read alone or used a guide for Bible study groups, *Beyond Expectations* will draw you deeper into the story of the King who came to save…
Not the way we imagined—but just as God had planned.

Step into the Kingdom.
Let it turn your expectations upside down.

*Available at Amazon, Barnes & Noble, and retailers across the nation.*

**Also from the author:**

## It's NOT Adam's Fault!

### A Decision in Carthage—
*...over 1,600 years ago still shapes our world today... if you can believe it.*

In *It's NOT Adam's Fault!*, the doctrine of inherited sin is questioned with clarity and conviction. What if sin isn't passed down, but is a personal choice? This book challenges "original sin" and offers a biblically grounded perspective on sin's true nature.

At the heart of this exploration is the Council of Carthage (418 AD), where the dogma of "original sin" was fused with infant baptism. What began as a theological decree became a power shift, used by the Roman Church to control monarchs, amass wealth, and dominate spiritual and temporal realms for centuries.

This wasn't just a doctrinal change—it was a historical turning point, one that reshaped Europe and beyond.

Through Scripture and church history, *It's NOT Adam's Fault!* reveals how a single, flawed translation altered Christian thought—and why Christ's freedom is far more radical and personal than we've been led to believe.

**Are you ready to challenge what you've been taught about sin, salvation, and the gospel?**

This perspective could change the way you see the world—and your place in it.

*Available at Amazon, Barnes & Noble, and retailers across the nation.*

# BIN TRAVERLER FORM

Cut By: _____Dora_____ #11 Qty _66_ Date _06-02-26_

Scanned By: _____ Qty _____ Date _____

Scanned Batch ID's

_____ _____

Notes / Exceptions

_____